James C. Oehlschläger

A Key to Ahn's Practical and Easy Method of Learning the German

Language

James C. Oehlschläger

A Key to Ahn's Practical and Easy Method of Learning the German Language

ISBN/EAN: 9783743359987

Manufactured in Europe, USA, Canada, Australia, Japa

Cover: Foto ©Paul-Georg Meister /pixelio.de

Manufactured and distributed by brebook publishing software
(www.brebook.com)

James C. Oehlschläger

A Key to Ahn's Practical and Easy Method of Learning the German

Language

A KEY

TO

'AHN'S

PRACTICAL AND EASY METHOD

OF

LEARNING

THE GERMAN LANGUAGE.

BY J. C. ŒHSCHLÆGER,

AUTHOR OF AN ENGLISH PRONOUNCING DICTIONARY FOR GERMANS, A GERMAN PRONOUNC-
ING DICTIONARY FOR ENGLISHMEN, A PRONOUNCING GERMAN READER, ETC.

ST. LOUIS, MO.
PUBLISHED BY FRANCIS SALER.
1863.

PART I.

PAGE 9. No. 1.

I am large (tall). Thou art small. He is old. She is good. We are young. You are rich. They are poor. Am I tall? Art thou tired? Is she sick? Is she young? Are we rich? Are you poor? Are you old?

PAGE 9. No. 2.

Ich bin klein. Du bist jung. Wir sind müde. Sie sind reich. Bist du krank? Ihr seid arm. Ist sie alt? Seid ihr krank? Sind sie gut? Er ist groß. Bin ich arm?

PAGE 9. No. 3.

Art thou wicked? I am not wicked. He is sad. We are not strong. Are they faithful? Art thou not happy? You are not industrious. She is not idle. Is he not tired? We are not poor. Are they not polite? Thou art not sick.

PAGE 9. No. 4.

Ich bin nicht groß. Sie sind faul. Sie ist nicht krank. Wir sind nicht glücklich. Er ist nicht klein. Seid ihr nicht müde? Sie sind nicht reich. Ist er nicht fleißig? Du bist nicht stark. Sie sind nicht glücklich. Er ist nicht höflich. Sind sie nicht treu? Ist sie nicht reich? Er ist nicht böse.

PAGE 10. No. 5.

The father is good. The mother is sad. The child is idle. The garden is not very long. The city is large and rich. The house is not high. Is the garden handsome? Is the father sick? Is the child not industrious? Is the house new? The father and the mother are happy.

PAGE 10. No. 6.

Das Haus ist nicht neu. Die Mutter und das Kind sind krank. Die Stadt ist sehr schön. Das Kind ist nicht unartig. Der Vater ist sehr alt. Das Haus und der Garten sind sehr groß. Ist die Mutter nicht glücklich? Das Haus ist nicht sehr alt. Ist der Garten nicht sehr schön? Das Haus ist sehr klein.

(3)

4

PAGE 10.   No. 7.

This man is very poor.   This window is very high.   This flower is beautiful.   This horse is young and strong.   Is this woman happy?   This father and this mother are not satisfied.   This tree is very large.   This woman is poor and sick.   This child is very naughty.   This man is not polite.   Art thou sad or ill?

PAGE 10.   No. 8.

Diese Frau ist müde.   Dieser Berg ist nicht hoch.   Ist dieses Kind artig oder unartig?   Dieser Mann ist nicht zufrieden.   Dieses Kind ist nicht sehr fleißig.   Ist dieser Garten klein oder groß?   Bist du nicht zufrieden?   Dieses Fenster ist nicht offen.   Ist dieses Haus alt oder neu?   Dieser Baum ist sehr schön.   Ist dieser Mann reich oder arm?   Diese Stadt ist sehr traurig (öde).

PAGE 10.   No. 9.

My brother is sad.   My sister is sick.   My book is handsome.   Is thy garden large?   Is thy pen good?   Is thy horse small?   Charles is still a child.   Berlin is a town.   Louisa is my sister.   Thy brother is my friend.   Thy father is not here.   Where is my book?   Is my book not here?   Is thy mother still sick?   I am not yet tired, but thy brother and sister are very tired.

PAGE 11.   No. 10.

Karl ist mein Bruder.   Dieses Kind ist meine Schwester.   Du bist mein Freund.   Dein Garten ist sehr groß.   Wo ist deine Mutter?   Ein Freund ist treu.   Ist dieses Kind dein Bruder?   Dieses Pferd ist noch jung.   Wo ist meine Feder?   Deine Feder ist hier.   Luise ist noch ein Kind.   Dein Bruder ist faul.   Mein Freund ist sehr fleißig.

PAGE 11.   No. 11.

Our garden is large.   Our mother is sick.   Our horse is beautiful.   This man is our father.   This woman is our mother.   Charles is your brother.   Louisa is your sister.   Is your son industrious?   Is your daughter contended?   Where is your book?   Our house is old.   Our door is always open.   This father and this mother are very sad; their son is always sick.

PAGE 11.   No. 12.

Unser Vater ist gut.   Unsere Mutter ist klein.   Unser Kind ist krank.   Ist dieser Mann Ihr Bruder?   Ist diese Frau Ihre Mutter?   Ihr Sohn ist nicht immer fleißig.   Ist Ihr Pferd schön?   Dieses Kind ist unser Bruder.   Ist Karl nicht euer Freund?   Luise ist nicht eure Schwester.

Page 11. No. 13.

My brother is older than I. I am younger than my friend. Charles is taller than Louisa. This man is taller than we. The dog is more faithful than the cat. The horse is more handsome and more useful than the dog. This child is more industrious than thou. You are happier than your brother. Charles is stronger than I. We are more contented than you. Louisa is more polite than thy sister. Is thy brother younger than thou? He is older, but smaller than I.

Page 12. No. 14.

Mein Bruder ift fleißiger als du. Du bift nicht jünger als er. Er ift größer und ftärker als ich. Ihr Sohn ift jünger als dieſes Kind. Der Mond ift kleiner als die Sonne. Bift du älter als ich? Dieſer Hund ift ſchöner als dieſe Katze. Ihre Schweſter ift höflicher als Sie. Ich bin zufriedener als Sie. Sie find reicher als wir. Wir find unglücklicher als Sie.

Page 12. No. 15.

My book is handsomer than that one. My pen is better than that one. Steel is harder than iron. This mountain is higher than that one. The cat is not as faithful as the dog. Lead is not so hard as iron. Is your house not bigger than that one? Is lead dearer than iron? The moon is not as big as the earth? This child is more diligent than that one. That woman is poorer than this one. Our garden is not so long and so beautiful as this one.

Page 12. No. 16.

Das Blei ift ſchwerer als das Eiſen. Dieſer Baum ift nicht ſo hoch als jener. Ift dieſes Buch nicht beſſer als jenes? Unſer Garten ift kleiner als dieſer. Dieſes Haus ift höher als jenes. Das Eiſen ift nützlicher als das Blei. Ich bin nicht ſo alt als er. Das Blei ift nicht ſo theuer als der Stahl. Unſere Stadt ift größer und ſchöner als dieſe. Wir find nicht ſo reich als dieſer Mann, aber wir find zufriedener als er.

Page 13. No. 17.

I am right. Thou art wrong. I have a book. Thou hast a pen. My brother has a watch. We have a house. You have a horse. Charles and Louisa have a cat. Hast thou a sister? Has this man a daughter? Have you a child? This watch is for my mother. This pen is for Charles. Have you still your mother? Why hast thou my knife? I have not thy knife.

Page 13. No. 18.

Karl, haſt du meine Feder? Luiſe, haſt du mein Buch? Heinrich hat deine Feder und Ludwig hat dein Buch. Du haſt Recht. Mein Sohn hat Unrecht. Wir haben ein Buch und eine Feder. Haben Sie auch ein Pferd und eine Uhr? Dieſes Meſſer iſt für Heinrich. Iſt dieſe Uhr für deine Mutter? Hat euer Freund ein Meſſer? Karl und Ludwig haben ein Pferd. Hat Ihr Vater noch eine Schweſter? Iſt dieſe Blume für meine Tochter?

Page 13. No. 19.

I have lost my book. Hast thou found my knife? I have not found thy knife. Have you my pen? We have not thy pen. My father has bought this horse. We have sold our house. Where hast thou found my watch? Why have you taken my watch? I have seen your mother and your sister. Why has your father not bought this house? Has thy brother taken my pen? He has not taken thy pen.

Page 13. No. 20.

Wo haſt du dieſes Buch gefunden? Haben Sie Ihre Feder verloren? Hat Ihr Vater dieſes Pferd gekauft? Warum haben Sie Ihre Uhr verkauft? Warum haben Sie nicht meine Feder genommen? Mein Bruder hat dein Meſſer gefunden. Wir haben deine Mutter geſehen. Ich habe dieſe Frau noch nicht geſehen. Karl und Ludwig haben ihre Mutter verloren, ſie ſind ſehr traurig.

Page 14. No. 21.

I have seen the king. Hast thou received the letter? My sister has not written the letter. Henry has lost the cane. My father has bought this house and (this) garden. Where have you found this dog and this cat? I have often before seen this man. Why have you taken this hat? We have found this letter. Has thy brother lost this cane?

Page 14. No. 22.

Wir haben das Haus und den Garten verkauft. Haben Sie dieſen Hund und dieſes Pferd gekauft? Ich habe den Mann und die Frau, den Sohn und die Tochter geſehen. Ich habe dieſen Brief nicht geſchrieben. Wo haben Sie dieſes Buch und dieſen Stock gefunden? Hat dein Bruder dieſen Baum gekauft? Dieſer Brief iſt für dieſen Mann. Haſt du dieſen Hut verloren? Haſt du nicht dieſes Buch und dieſe Feder genommen? Haſt du ſchon den König geſehen? Ich habe den König noch nicht geſehen.

7

Page 14. No. 23.

My brother is very much pleased, he has a bird. Hast thou received a letter? I have lost my hat. Have you already seen my dog? We have bought a table and a chair. My brother has taken thy cane. Where hast thou bought thy pencil? We have lost our father and our mother. I have not received your letter. Has thy brother already seen our garden and our house? Our neighbor has seen the king. Hast thou bought this bird or that one?

Page 14. No. 24.

Wir haben unſern Hund verloren. Dieſer Mann hat einen Sohn und eine Tochter verloren. Wo haben Sie meinen Bleiſtift gefunden? Haben Sie ſchon meinen Bruder und meine Mutter geſehen? Ich habe einen Hut für meine Schweſter gekauft. Unſer Nachbar hat dein Meſſer und deinen Stock gefunden. Wo haſt du dieſen Tiſch gekauft? Dein Bruder hat meinen Stuhl genommen. Haben Sie einen Brief geſchrie= ben. Wir haben dieſen Stock und jenen gefunden.

Page 15. No. 25.

My friend is sad, his father and his mother are sick. My aunt is satisfied; her son and her daughter are very industrious. Henry has lost his cane, his watch and his knife. Louisa has lost her thimble, her pen and her book. Your uncle has sold his house and his garden. This woman has lost her husband and her child. This daughter has written a letter for her mother. Charles (has not known) did not know his father. The aunt has written thy letter and mine.

Page 15. No. 26.

Der Vater hat ſeinen Sohn verloren. Dieſe Mutter hat ihre Tochter verloren. Mein Onkel hat ſeine Uhr verkauft. Unſere Tante hat ihre Scheeren verkauft. Heinrich hat ſeinen Bleiſtift gefunden. Luiſe hat ihren Fingerhut gefunden. Ich habe dieſen Mann und ſeinen Sohn, dieſe Frau und ihre Tochter geſehen. Meine Mutter hat ihre Feder und ihr Meſſer verloren. Mein Bruder hat ſeinen Hut genommen. Ich habe Ihre Tante geſehen, hat ſie noch ihr Pferd? Dieſer Mann iſt ſehr traurig, er hat ſeine Frau verloren. Karl hat einen Brief für ſeinen Vater geſchrieben. Meine Tante hat dieſes Buch für ihren Sohn gekauft.

Page 15. No. 27.

The mother of the Queen has arrived. The father of the neighbor (f.) is departed. I have seen the garden of the aunt. Have you found the pencil of the sister. This woman is the sister of the neighbor (f.). This man is the brother of the servant-maid. The child of this woman is always sick.

Page 16.   No. 28.

Der Hut der Mutter ist schön.   Die Schwester der Königin ist nicht schön.   Ist der Vater der Magd angekommen?   Sind Sie der Bruder der Nachbarin?   Ich bin die Schwester dieser Frau.   Hast du den Stuhl der Schwester genommen?   Haben Sie das Pferd der Tante gesehen? Wir haben den Vater dieser Magd gekannt.

Page 16.   No. 29.

The servant (*f.*) of the tailor is sick.   The son of the neighbor is still very young.   The flower of the gardener is very beautiful. The king's garden is very large.   The king is the father of the people.   The wife of the physician is always contented.   I have seen the uncle's garden.   We have bought the merchant's house. Hast thou taken the pencil of the brother?   Where is the maid-servant of the shoemaker?   The door of the room is always open. The daughter of this man is departed.   We have known the mother of this child.   The garden of this house is small.

Page 16.   No. 30.

Dieser Mann ist der Bruder des Gärtners.   Diese Frau ist die Schwester des Schuhmachers.   Dieses Kind ist der Sohn des Schnei= ders.   Die Thür des Hauses ist nicht offen.   Ich habe den Sohn und die Tochter des Arztes gesehen.   Wir haben das Pferd des Kaufmanns gesehen.   Die Magd des Nachbars ist die Schwester dieses Gärtners. Warum ist die Thür dieses Zimmers offen?   Wir haben den Sohn dieses Kaufmanns gekannt.   Der Hund des Nachbars ist treu.   Die Mutter dieses Kindes ist angekommen.

Page 16.   No. 31.

Are you the son of the physician?   I am the son of a merchant. Have you bought the house of my neighbor?   The brother of thy friend has arrived yesterday.   Where is the umbrella of thy uncle? Hast thou seen the room of my sister?   We have read the letter of thy mother.   My uncle has bought your father's house.   I have lost your brother's cane.   The garden of our neighbor is very large. Our servant-girl is the daughter of your gardener.   Where is the umbrella of our mother?   Charles has taken the thimble of his sister.   Louisa has taken her aunt's penknife.

Page 17.   No. 32.

Ich habe den Hut eines Kindes gefunden.   Sind Sie die Magd meines Onkels?   Ich bin die Magd Ihres Schneiders.   Das Feder= messer deines Bruders ist sehr gut.   Die Feder deiner Schwester ist nicht gut. Das Haus unserer Tante ist groß. Heinrich hat den Brief seines Vaters verloren. Luise hat die Feder ihres Bruders gefunden. Ist der Garten unseres Onkels so schön als dieser? Wir haben den Hut des Sohnes Ihres Nachbarn gefunden. Ludwig hat den Brief seines Freundes gelesen. Luise hat eine Blume für ein Kind ihrer Schwester gekauft.

PAGE 17. No. 33.

This house belongs to my neighbor's uncle. That garden belongs to my friend's aunt. I have written a letter to the father. She has given a flower to the friend (*f.*) of her sister. Charles has lent his penknife to the sister. Hast thou sent my book to the physician? I have promised a bird to this child. Henry has lent this woman our umbrella. Louisa has shown our garden to this man. I have given my pen to the friend of my brother.

PAGE 17. No. 34.

Der Hut gehört dem Gärtner. Dieses Haus gehört der Mutter meines Freundes. Ich habe meinem Onkel und meiner Tante geschrieben. Meine Schwester hat ihren Fingerhut der Freundin Ihres Bruders geliehen. Mein Onkel hat eine Uhr dem Sohne Ihrer Nachbarin geschickt. Haben Sie dem Kinde einen Stuhl gegeben? Haben Sie dieser Frau einen Regenschirm geliehen? Gehört dieser Garten dem Könige? Nein, er gehört der Schwester des Königs. Wir haben unser Pferd dem Freunde unseres Onkels verkauft. Gehört dieses Messer dieser oder jener Magd?

PAGE 18. No. 35.

This garden belongs to a shoemaker. This knife belongs to a servant (*f.*). Louisa has written a letter to my father. Henry has given a flower to my mother. I have lent my horse to your uncle. They have sold their house to our aunt. Charles has sent a book to his friend. Amelia has lent a thimble to her friend (*f.*). This man has sent a bird to your neighbor. Hast thou given this watch to my father? Have you lent a pencil to our cousin (*f.*)?

PAGE 18. No. 36.

Ich habe meine Feder einem Freunde meines Bruders geliehen. Hast du deine Katze einer Freundin meiner Schwester gegeben? Wir haben den Brief einer Magd des Doctors gegeben. Haben Sie diese Blume unserm Gärtner geschickt? Dieser Garten gehört meinem Vetter (meiner Base). Dieser Regenschirm gehört nicht Ihrem Bruder. Gehört diese Feder deinem Bruder oder deiner Schwester? Hat Heinrich seinem Vater oder seiner Mutter geschrieben? Hat Luise ihrem Onkel oder ihrer Tante geschrieben?

Page 18. No. 37.

I hâve seen the book of the physician. Have you received the book from the physician? We have bought the garden of our neighbor. Have you bought this garden from your neighbor? I have received this watch from my uncle. Henry has received a letter from his father and mother. I am speaking of the King and of the Queen. We are speaking of your brother and of your sister; of this man and of this woman. Are you speaking of my cousin (m.) or of my female cousin? Henry is loved by his father and mother.

Page 19. No. 38.

Ich habe dieſes Pferd von meinem Freunde erhalten. Ich habe dieſe Katze von deiner Schweſter gekauft. Luiſe hat einen Regenſchirm von ihrem Onkel und eine Uhr von ihrer Tante erhalten. Ich ſpreche von dieſem Hunde und von dieſer Katze, von dieſem Vogel und von dieſer Blume. Wir ſprechen von ihrem Vetter (von Ihrer Baſe). Amalie wird von ihrem Onkel und (von) ihrer Tante geliebt. Unſers Gärtners Frau hat einen Brief von ihrem Sohne und ihrer Tochter erhalten. Heinrich iſt der Sohn dieſes Schuhmachers und Luiſe iſt die Tochter dieſes Schneiders.

Page 19. No. 39.

The cat is not so strong as the dog. The lion is stronger than the tiger. The lion is the strongest animal. My neighbor is richer than you; he is the richest man in the town. Gold is heavier than silver. Iron is more useful than silver. Iron is the most useful metal. Louisa is more beautiful than Amelia; but Henry is the handsomest child. Lewis is younger than thou; he is the youngest son of our neighbor. Charles is older than I; he is the oldest son of my uncle. The dog is very faithful. The dog is the most faithful animal. This book is better than that one. Thou art the best friend of my brother. The house of this merchant is the highest in the town.

Page 19. No. 40.

Dieſer Vogel iſt ſehr klein; es iſt der kleinſte Vogel. Luiſe iſt ſehr ſchön; ſie iſt ſchöner als ihre Schweſter. Das Silber iſt nicht ſo nütz= lich als das Eiſen. Der Tiger iſt nicht ſo ſtark als der Löwe. Der Schneider iſt der glücklichſte Mann in der Stadt. Heinrich iſt fleißiger als Ludwig, aber Karl iſt der fleißigſte. Dein Regenſchirm iſt ſehr ſchön; der Regenſchirm meines Vetters iſt der ſchönſte. Sie ſind nicht ſo arm als mein Vetter; er iſt der ärmſte Mann in der Stadt. Mein Stuhl iſt zu hoch; dieſer iſt höher; aber der Stuhl meiner Mutter iſt der höchste. Ich habe meinem Bruder den besten Bleistift und die beste Feder gegeben.

PAGE 20. No. 41.

Who is there? It is the tailor; it is Henry; it is I. Who is that man? It is the shoemaker; it is the son of the physician. Who has written this letter? To whom does this dog belong? He belongs to our neighbor. To whom does this watch belong? It belongs to my sister. To whom have you given the hat? From whom have you received this flower? Whom have you seen? What have you lost? I have lost nothing. Have you found something? Where is your brother? He is not here. Is somebody there? Nobody is there. Has somebody taken my pen? Nobody has taken your pen.

PAGE 20. No. 42.

Wer ist da? Es ist mein Schneider; es ist Karl. Wer ist diese Frau? Es ist die Frau des Schuhmachers; es ist die Magd des Nachbars. Wem haben Sie Ihr Messer geliehen? Dem Sohne des Gärtners. Wem hat Ihr Bruder seinen Hund verkauft? Der Schwester meines Freundes. Von wem hast du diesen Vogel erhalten? Von dem Vater dieses Mädchens. Was haben Sie gekauft? Ich habe einen Regenschirm für meine Base gekauft. Was haben Sie genommen? Ich habe nichts genommen. Von wem sprechen Sie? Ich spreche von Niemandem. Hat Jemand meinen Brief gelesen? Niemand hat Ihren Brief gelesen.

PAGE 20. No. 43.

What cabinet-maker has made this table? What servant-girl has written this letter? What child has cried (wept)? Which dog have you bought? Which watch hast thou lost? Which house has your father sold? Of what nation are you speaking? With what friend didst thou go out? In what garden has he found the bird? Which pen hast thou? To what woman hast thou given thy knife? To which girl hast thou lent thy thimble? At what merchant's have you bought this pencil? With what pen have you written this letter? With whom have you arrived?

PAGE 21. No. 44.

Wo ist Ihre Schwester? Sie ist in Ihrem Garten. Wo ist Ihr Bruder? Er ist bei seinem Freunde. Ist Ihr Vater ausgegangen? Er ist mit dem Doctor ausgegangen. Welchen Hut haben Sie gekauft? Welches Buch haben Sie gelesen? Welche Feder haben Sie genommen? Welcher Knabe ist der fleißigste? Welche Uhr ist die beste? Von

welchem Gärtner haft du diese Blume erhalten? Bei welcher Frau haft
du diesen Vogel gekauft? In welchem Hause haben Sie Ihren Fingerhut
verloren? Mit wem ist Ihr Bruder abgereist? Welchem Manne haben
Sie Ihren Regenschirm geliehen? Welchen Stock haben Sie verloren?
Welcher Schreiner hat diesen Tisch gemacht?

PAGE 21.   No. 45.

We have a brother who is very tall. You have a sister who is
very small. My son has a book which is very useful. The garden,
which thy uncle has bought, is very beautiful. The pen, which
my cousin has found, is very good. I have seen the house, which
your father has bought. Have you found the thimble, which my
sister has lost? Hast thou eaten the apple, which thou hast found?
I have eaten the pear, which I have bought. Here is the man, to
whom you have given your letter. Here is the woman, to whom
we have sold our dog. Here is the physician, of whom we speak
so often.

PAGE 21.   No. 46.

Ich habe einen Hund, der sehr klein ist. Wir haben eine Katze, welche
sehr schön ist. Mein Vater hat ein Haus gekauft, welches sehr schön ist.
Haben Sie den Regenschirm gesehen, den meine Mutter gekauft hat?
Hast du die Birne gefunden, die dein Bruder verloren hat? Wir haben
das Pferd gesehen, welches (das) Ihr Onkel verkauft hat. Wo ist der
Fingerhut, den Sie gefunden haben? Ich habe den Bleistift genommen,
welchen (den) mein Vetter gekauft hat? Heinrich hat den Apfel gegessen,
den sein Bruder empfangen hat. Haben Sie die Frau gesehen, von der
wir sprechen? Haben Sie den Brief gelesen, den ich geschrieben habe?
Haben Sie den Knaben gefunden, welchem dieses Federmesser gehört?

PAGE 22.   No. 47.

He who is contented, is rich. This thimble is better than that
of my sister. This watch is smaller than that of thy brother. This
house is handsomer than that of our neighbor. I have lost my
hat and that of my cousin. We have found thy pen and that of
thy friend. Henry has seen my room and that of my uncle. Hast
thou taken my cane or that of my brother? That is not thy flower,
it is that of my mother. Have you my knife or that of the gardener? Do you speak of my son or of that of the physician? The
horse, which we have bought, is younger than that of your father.

PAGE 22.   No. 48.

Derjenige, welcher reich ist, ist nicht immer zufrieden. Mein Hund ist
treuer als der meines Oheims. Unsere Magd ist stärker als diejenige (die)
unseres Nachbars. Mein Zimmer ist größer als dasjenige (das) meines

Freundes. Dieser Regenschirm ist schöner als derjenige (der), welchen wir gekauft haben. Haben Sie meine Feder, oder die meiner Schwester genommen? Dieses ist nicht Ihr Bleistift, es ist derjenige meines Bruders. Ich spreche von meinem Buche und von dem Ihres Freundes. Luise hat ihren Fingerhut und den ihrer Mutter verloren. Du hast meinen Apfel und den meines Vetters gegessen. Meine Uhr ist besser als diejenige meiner Base. Ich habe Ihren Brief und den Ihres Bruders erhalten.

PAGE 22. No. 49.

My brother's name is Henry, and that of my sister is Louisa. The father of William is arrived. The mother of Louisa is departed. The uncle of Lewis is very rich. Emily's bonnet is very handsome. Have you received this dog from Henry or from Ferdinand? Amelia has lent her pen to John. Charles has given a flower to Emily. Does this garden belong to Lewis or to Caroline? Where is William? He is gone out with Charles and Joseph. Does your uncle reside in Brussels or in Paris? Is your cousin going to Vienna or to Berlin? Is Paris larger than Lyons? Is your friend a native of Cologne or of Aix la Chapelle?

PAGE 23. No. 50.

Mein Vetter heißt Johann. Die Tochter der Frau unseres Gärtners heißt Johanna. Bist du Karl's oder Ferdinand's Bruder? Wo sind Heinrich und Ludwig? Sie sind in meines Vaters Zimmer; sie sind mit Wilhelm ausgegangen. Haben Sie Ihre Feder dem Heinrich geliehen? Wer hat diese Blume der Luise gegeben? Wir haben einen Brief von Ludwig erhalten; er ist in Düsseldorf. Die Schwester Karl's ist sehr klein. Josephinens Hut ist sehr groß. Mein Oheim wohnt in Wien, und mein Vetter in Paris. Mein Freund geht nach Köln. Wilhelm ist von Amsterdam angekommen. Haben Sie den Johann und den Ludwig gesehen? Mein Garten ist größer als derjenige der Emilie. Luise ist mit ihrer Mutter ausgegangen. Heinrich ist mit seinem Freunde Ferdinand abgereist.

PART II.

PAGE 23. No. 51.

The friends of my father have arrived. The sons of our neighbor are very industrious. The chairs, which we have bought, are very beautiful. Have you seen the towns of Vienna and of Berlin? Charles has found the hats of William and of Ferdinand. My father has not received the letters of your uncle. Iron and silver are metals. Horses are more useful than dogs. The servant-girls of your neighbor are very industrious. The physicians in this town are very rich. To whom have you given the canes of my brother? The animals, which we have seen in your garden, are very strong. Have you written to the friends of Henry? Give this dog to the sons of my brother. We are speaking of the letters of the physician.

Page 24. No. 52.

Dein Bruder hat die Hunde meines Nachbars gekauft. Die Freunde Karl's sind krank. Haben Sie die Pferde unseres Oheims gesehen? Wer hat die Briefe meines Bruders geschrieben? Wo sind die Hüte, welche Sie gekauft haben? Ich habe diesen Vogel von den Söhnen dieses Arztes erhalten. Ich habe Ihren Regenschirm den Mägden gegeben. Die Metalle sind sehr nützlich. Die Hunde sind sehr treu. Ihr Bruder ist mit den Söhnen unserer Nachbarin ausgegangen. Köln und Aachen sind Städte. Ich spreche von Heinrich's und Wilhelm's Freunden.

Page 24. No. 53.

My teeth are very white. I have very warm feet. Your hands are not clean. Has the shoemaker brought my shoes? Who has taken my stockings? Are these your stockings? These are not my sister's. Where have you bought these nuts? Have you already seen my trees? Of which trees are you speaking? Of those which I have bought of the king's gardener. Our friends have already departed. Who has written these letters? My father has sold his houses and his dogs. My neighbor has received a letter from his sons, who are in Berlin. Has anybody found my rings? Nobody has seen thy rings. Charles is beloved by his friends.

Page 24. No. 54.

Karl und Heinrich haben ihre Stöcke verloren. Der Schuhmacher hat Ihre Schuhe nicht gemacht. Wo haben Sie diese Tische und Stühle gekauft? Von wem haben Sie diese Bleistifte erhalten? Meine Füße sind sehr klein. Meine Schwester hat ihre Fingerhüte verloren. Ich habe diese Briefe von meinen Freunden erhalten. Diese Bäume sind höher als jene. Diese Thiere sind sehr schön. Diese Mägde sind sehr faul. Haben Sie schon unsere Hüte und unsere Ringe gesehen? Emiliens Strümpfe sind weißer als die der Luise. Ihre Zähne sind nicht rein. Meine Hände sind sehr warm. Ich habe diese Nüsse in meines Oheims Garten gefunden.

Page 25. No. 55.

These houses are higher than those. Those ribbons are finer than these. Thy books are more useful than those of Louisa. This mother has lost her children. The king has sold his castles. From whom have you obtained these glasses? Who has made these clothes? This man is already very old; he has lost all his teeth. Where are your friends? All my friends are gone out. These nations are very happy; they have a king, who is very good. Kings are not always happy. Henry and William have lost all their books. All your letters have arrived. We have found all these nuts in the forest of our uncle. The father has set out with all his children. These villages are very beautiful. Of which villages are you speaking? What towns have you seen? Are all these stockings for Louisa or for Emily? Have you given the children of the neighbor a bird? Who has made all these holes in my table?

Page 25. No. 56.

Wo sind Ihre Kinder? Meine Kinder sind ausgegangen. Ihre Freunde sind angekommen. Haben Sie noch nicht Ihre Briefe geschrieben? Wer hat alle diese Bänder gekauft? Henriette hat alle diese Bücher verloren. Wir haben alle diese Häuser gesehen. Haben Sie auch die Schlösser des Königs gesehen? Wer hat alle meine Nüsse genommen? Diese Kinder haben ihre Hüte verloren. Gib diese Gläser dem Heinrich, und diese Ringe der Luise. Dieser Baum hat alle seine Blätter verloren. Mein Nachbar hat alle seine Hühner verkauft.

Page 26. No. 57.

The tailors and shoemakers in this town are all rich. The English are all industrious. My brothers are all sick. Have you seen my sisters? Where have you bought these knives, forks and spoons? The windows of your room are open. Charles and Henry are my cousins. We have found these birds in the forest. Tigers are very strong. These girls are very happy. Are my daughters gone out? Are my rooms not very handsome? Has your aunt bought all these looking-glasses? Who has taken the books and pens of this girl? To whom do these gardens and houses belong? Louisa and Henrietta have lost their pins. The shoemaker has not yet brought your shoes and your boots. Who are those men? They are Italians; they are the uncles of my friend. These mothers are very sad; they have lost all their children.

Page 26. No. 58.

Der Schuhmacher hat Ihre Schuhe und Stiefeln gebracht. Die Häuser dieses Dorfes sind alle sehr schön. Bringen Sie uns die Löffel, Gabeln und Messer. Wo haben Sie diese Nadeln gekauft? Ihre Brüder und Schwestern sind nicht gekommen. Ludwig und Ferdinand sind Vettern. Unsere Mütter haben die Gärten des Königs gesehen. Meine

Söhne haben die Spiegel von meinem Nachbar gekauft. Die Pferde sind größer als die Tiger. Sind meine Strümpfe rein? Sind Ihre Schuhe neu?

PAGE 26. No. 59.

In our house there are fourteen rooms. In this room there are two tables and twelve chairs. Our neighbor has five children: three sons and two daughters. We have four cats and three dogs. In your garden there are fifteen trees. A year has twelve months; a month has four weeks; a week has seven days. I have received from my father six apples and eight pears. My uncle has given to my sister a penknife and twenty pens. Hast thou already done all thy exercises? John has not yet done his exercise. My brother *has been* in Berlin these three years. Have you not yet dined? I dined three hours ago. Has your father not yet arrived? He arrived as early as two days ago. My uncle *has been* sick these four weeks; he has eaten nothing for the last week. My brother is nine years old, but my sister is not yet seven (years old).

PAGE 27. No. 60.

Mein Vater hat drei Häuser und zwei Gärten. Dieser Mann hat fünf Knaben und vier Mädchen. Mein Freund hat sieben Schwestern. Wir haben sechs Briefe erhalten. In der Stadt gibt es zwanzig Aerzte. Meine Basen haben zwei Katzen gekauft. Mein Vetter ist siebzehn Jahre und zwei Monate alt. Meine Mutter hat sechs Messer, zwölf Gabeln und achtzehn Löffel gekauft. Unser Schreiner hat drei Tische und zehn Stühle gemacht. Wir haben diese Woche fünfzehn Hühner und drei Kälber erhalten. Wilhelm hat fünf Aepfel, vier Birnen und elf Nüsse gegessen. Heinrich ist seit drei Tagen angekommen. Mein Oheim ist seit einem Jahre abgereist. Karl und Ferdinand haben Aufgaben geschrieben. Es sind zwei Löcher in dieser Thür. Der Gärtner hat meinen Kindern drei Blumen gegeben.

PAGE 27. No. 61.

I have eaten bread and meat. We have bought cherries and plums. My brother has drunk wine, and you have drunk beer and water. The shoemaker makes boots and shoes. The cabinet-maker makes tables and chairs. At this merchant's are found (one finds) books, pens, ink and pencils. Give me soup and vegetables. Here is wine and water, and there is coffee and milk. Have you also sugar? We have bought knives and forks, cups and glasses. The gardener has given cherries and flowers to Louisa. Have you already taken your coffee? In that house we find looking-glasses, umbrellas, ribbons, thimbles and needles. My friend (*f.*) has received pears and nuts from her uncle. We have seen lions, tigers, cats and dogs. In this town there are tailors and shoemakers, who are very rich.

PAGE 28. No. 62.

Wollen Sie Wein oder Bier, Milch oder Wasser? Geben Sie mir gefälligst Suppe, Gemüse, Fleisch und Brot. Wo findet man Dinte und Federn? Sind Sie ein Vater? Haben Sie Kinder? Hat Ihr Vater Bäume oder Blumen gekauft? Mein Bruder hat Bücher und Freunde. Hier ist Kaffee und Zucker. Mein Nachbar hat Vögel, Hunde und Pferde. Wir sprechen von Städten und Dörfern, von Häusern und Gärten. Das Eisen und das Silber sind Metalle. Wien und Berlin sind Städte. Was haben Sie gemacht? Wir haben Aufgaben gemacht. Wir haben Briefe geschrieben. Wir haben Aepfel und Pflaumen gegessen, und wir haben Wein und Bier getrunken.

PAGE 28. No. 63.

Henry has much money; he has more money than I. Give me a little meat. I have bread enough. Thou hast too much salt and pepper. We have less fruit than you. Louisa has fewer pens than Henrietta. Charles has done more exercises than Lewis. Hast thou as much money as my brother? The poor man has few friends. There are few men who are contented. Do not give Henrietta too much mustard. My brother has drunk too much wine. This mother has many children. This man has many flowers. How many dogs has your father? There are few cherries this year, but a great many plums. My friend has received this week more letters than I. Has thy father as many books as my uncle? Please (to) give me a little ink. Will you have some more? I have enough.

PAGE 28. No. 64.

Es giebt viel Obst dieses Jahr. Unser Gärtner hat viele Bäume und Blumen. Wollen Sie ein wenig Fleisch oder Gemüse haben? Haben Sie genug Senf? Ich habe genug Salz und Pfeffer. Unser Nachbar hat viel Geld, er ist sehr reich. Geben Sie der Frau ein wenig Wein. Dieser Mann hat wenig Freunde, aber er hat viel Hunde und Katzen. Es sind viele Vögel in diesem Walde. Wie viel Aerzte gibt es in Ihrer Stadt? Haben Sie so viele Aepfel und Birnen als wir? Wir haben nicht so viele als Sie, aber wir haben mehr Pflaumen und Nüsse als Sie. Karl hat weniger Freunde als Heinrich. Dieser Baum hat weniger Blätter als jener. Es sind zu viele Stühle in diesem Zimmer.

PAGE 29. No. 65.

My mother has sent Henrietta three pair of gloves, six pair of stockings, two dozen of shirts and a basket of cherries. In this trunk there are ten yards of linen, four pocket-handkerchiefs and

2

six stocks. My brother has bought two pair of shoes and a pair of boots. We have sent the friend of our uncles twenty pounds of sugar and ten bottles of wine. Give me a piece of cheese, a bottle of beer and a little mustard. I have drunk a glass of wine and have eaten a piece of ham. We have taken a cup of coffee with our friend (*f*.). Give me a glass of water and a piece of sugar. My sister has bought two pounds of cherries and a pound of plums. We have bought a dozen of chairs at the cabinet-maker's of our uncle. I have received a basket of flowers from the gardener.

PAGE 29. No. 66.

Der Schuhmacher hat ein Paar Schuhe für Luise, und zwei Paar Stiefeln für Wilhelm gemacht. Wir haben zwei Gläser Wein und drei Gläser Bier getrunken. Geben Sie mir eine Flasche Wasser und ein wenig Fleisch und Brot. Wollen Sie ein Stück Schinken oder Käse haben? Meine Tante hat ein Dutzend Halsbinden, zwei Dutzend Hemden und zehn Paar Handschuhe und Strümpfe gekauft. Wie viele Hemden haben Sie? Ich habe drei Dutzend. Diese Leinwand ist sehr fein; wie viele Ellen haben Sie gekauft? Ich habe zwanzig Ellen gekauft. Das ist nicht genug für zehn Hemden. Mein Oheim hat dem Heinrich ein Federmesser, zwanzig Federn, zwei Halsbinden und ein Paar Handschuhe gegeben. Ferdinand hat ein Pfund Pflaumen, sechs Pfund Kaffee und zwei Ellen Band gekauft. Geben Sie mir gefälligst ein Glas Wasser.

PAGE 30. No. 67.

Here is good ham, good soup and good bread. Have you good paper and good ink? We have drunk bad wine and good beer. Our gardener has excellent fruit. Our servant has bought good mustard, but bad pepper. Edward has good friends and useful books. My uncle has beautiful gardens and large houses. Your neighbor has faithful dogs. John give me a glass of water. Do you wish cold or warm water? My sister has bought a handsome pair of gloves. Your brother is always talking of good wine and good soup, but not of useful books, of exercises and of business. Paris and London are beautiful towns. Henry has received a pair of new shoes.

PAGE 30. No. 68.

Haben Sie guten Senf? Wir haben gutes Brot und gutes Fleisch. Ihr Gärtner hat sehr schöne Blumen. Diese Kinder haben schöne Kleider. Wir haben treue Freunde, liebenswürdige Brüder und nützliche Bücher. Geben Sie mir besseren Käse und besseres Bier. Bei diesem Kaufmanne findet man hübsche Handschuhe, schöne Federmesser und gute Federn. Das Eisen und das Silber sind sehr nützliche Metalle. Sie haben immer vortrefflichen Wein. Mein Bruder ist nicht ausgegangen,

er hat zu viele Geschäfte. Heinrich hat gutes Papier und gute Dinte ge=
kauft. Wir sprechen von gutem Kaffee, von vortrefflicher Frucht und
neuen Anzügen.

PAGE 30. No. 69.

Our gardener is a good man. Your gardener woman is a good
woman. Emily is a good child. We have a good father and a
good mother. Henry has a fine horse and a fine dog. Louisa has
large teeth, but a small hand and a small foot. Ferdinand is gone
out with my younger brother. Henrietta has departed with my
elder sister. Give this bread to a poor child. This penknife belongs to a young man, who lives with our neighbor. Lewis is the
son of a rich merchant. Have you any good wine or good beer?
We have no good wine and no good beer. Who has taken my
silver watch and my gold ring? We have lost our best friend.
Your little children are very healthy. There are no good cherries
this year. My uncle has sold his finest horses. Are you satisfied
with your new boots? Hast thou already eaten of our good plums?

PAGE 31. No. 70.

Karl ist ein guter Knabe. Henriette ist ein hübsches Mädchen. Das
ist eine glückliche Mutter. Das ist ein vortrefflicher Wein. Wo ist mein
kleiner Heinrich, meine gute Luise? Wir haben einen sehr reichen Oheim.
Wilhelm hat einen alten Vater. Das Eisen ist ein nützliches Metall. Der
Hund ist ein treues Thier. Ich habe einen neuen Regenschirm und eine
goldene Uhr erhalten. Mein Nachbar hat dieses Jahr viele Geschätfe ge=
macht. Geben Sie diese Flasche Wein einem armen Manne oder einer
armen Frau. Ich habe keine Freunde in dieser Stadt. Haben Sie keine
guten Federn für dieses Kind? Unsere besten Freunde sind todt. Der
Schreiner macht keine guten Stühle.

PAGE 31. No. 71.

Good Henry is sick. Little Sophia is very amiable. That poor
child has lost its mother. That is the highest tree in our garden.
Lisetta is the most industrious of our servants. This rich Eng-
lishman lives with my uncle. Where have you found this golden
pin? To whom does this large house and that beautiful garden
belong? Francis is gone out with little Charles. We have yesterday eaten cherries at (our) good Emily's. Who lives in this beautiful castle? What is the name of this beautiful flower? Where
have you bought this bad wine and this bad beer? I love industrious pupils and faithful friends. The lion and the tiger are
the strongest animals. Those are the happiest days of my life.
Give this poor man a little wine. Lend this poor girl your umbrella.

PAGE 31. No. 72.

Der fleißige Schüler wird von Jedermann geliebt. Das faule Kind wird von Niemandem geliebt. Der gute König wird von seinem Volke geliebt. Diese arme Frau hat kein Brod für ihre Kinder. Dieser reiche Kaufmann hat den Armen viel Geld gegeben. Ich liebe die hübschen Blumen und die hübschen Kinder. Ich liebe die schönen Anzüge nicht. Diese Frucht ist nicht gesund. Mein Bruder hat heute diesen goldenen Ring gefunden. Ludwig ist mit seinem kleinen Bruder ausgegangen. Der Vater dieses jungen Mannes ist ein Schuhmacher. Die Tochter dieser alten Frau ist krank. Haben Sie von diesem vortrefflichen Weine getrunken? Wollen Sie einige dieser schönen Pflaumen haben? Welchen Hut haben Sie genommen? Ich habe den weißen Hut genommen. Welche Uhr haben Sie verkauft? Ich habe die silberne Uhr verkauft.

PAGE 32. No. 73.

This young man is very industrious, he is the first of his class. Charles is the second; modest Henry the third; John is the fourth; little William is the fifth; Paul is the sixth; Francis is the eighth; Gustavus is the ninth; naughty Edward is the eleventh, and lazy Lewis the last. Two is the fifth part of ten. Five is the fourth part of twenty. One day is the seventh part of a week. What day of the month is this? This is the thirteenth or fourteenth. Is it not the twentieth? My father has departed on the third of May. My uncle has arrived the tenth of December. Have you the first volume and the second? I have only the first.

PAGE 32. No. 74.

Luise ist die erste in der Classe; Marie ist die zweite; die gute Josephine ist die dritte; Henriette ist die fünfte; die bescheidene Sophie ist die neunte; Mathilde ist die funfzehnte; die unartige Karoline ist die letzte. Drei ist der sechste Theil von achtzehn. Eine Woche ist der vierte Theil des Monats, und ein Monat ist der zwölfte Theil des Jahres. Den wievielsten haben wir? Es ist heute der elfte oder der zwölfte. Wir reisten am zweiten Mai ab, und kamen am sechzehnten an. Welchen Band haben Sie genommen? Haben Sie den dritten und vierten genommen? Ich habe nur den dritten genommen.

PAGE 32. No. 75.

Thy father is taller than mine. My mother is smaller than thine. Our book is more useful than yours. My son is not so old as thine. Your horse is younger than ours. Our books are more useful than yours. My father has lost his watch; Henry has also lost his. My sister has sold hers. My father has read thy letter and mine. My aunt has sold her garden and ours. Has my brother

taken my cane or his? Has Louisa found my thimble or hers?
Thy exercises are easier than mine. These trees are higher than
ours. In our town there are more physicians than in yours.

PAGE 33. No. 76.

Mein Fingerhut ist so schön als der Ihrige. Ihr Regenschirm ist nicht
so groß als meiner. Mein Sohn ist fleißiger, als der deinige (deiner).
Mein Freund hat sein Pferd und das meinige verkauft. Meine Schwester
hat ihren Apfel und den deinigen (deinen) gegessen. Hat Luise meine Fe=
der oder die ihrige genommen; meinen Bleistift oder den ihrigen? Hein=
rich hat meine Bücher und die Ihrigen gelesen. Ihre Schwestern sind
jünger als die unsrigen. Wir sprechen von unserm Freunde und von dem
Ihrigen. Ist mein Zimmer kleiner als das deinige (deines)? Ich habe
Ihrem Sohne und dem meinigen, Ihrer Tochter und der meinigen ein
Buch versprochen. Ich spreche von meinen Aufgaben und von den deini=
gen (deinen). Dieses Schloß gehört meinem Oheim und dem Ihrigen.

PAGE 33. No. 77.

Have you my cane? Yes, I have it. Have you my watch?
No, I have it not. Have you my knife? I have it not. Have you
my shoes? Yes, I have them. Where is my dog? I have not
seen him. Who has taken my pen? Thy brother has taken it.
Where hast thou found this pocket-book? I have found it in your
room. These birds are very beautiful. From whom hast thou
received them? Thy sister is very industrious; my mother is very
fond of her. Did you know my uncle? I did not know him. This
is a useful book, have you already read it? Where is my thimble?
I have given it to your sister; she has lost it. Has anybody taken
my fork? Charles has taken it. To whom has the gardener sent
all these flowers? He has sent them to your mother. Has Henry
had thy pencil? No, he has not had it to-day.

PAGE 33. No. 78.

Hat der Schuhmacher meinen Stiefel gebracht? Ja er hat ihn ge=
bracht. Hast du schon deine Aufgabe gemacht? Ich habe sie noch nicht
gemacht. Haben Sie mein neues Zimmer gesehen? Nein, ich habe es
noch nicht gesehen. Wo hast du diese schönen Ringe gekauft? Ich habe
sie in Paris gekauft. Wer hat mein Federmesser gehabt? Ich habe es
nicht gehabt, Ihr Bruder hat es gehabt. Ich habe einen Brief von mei=
ner Tante erhalten, haben Sie ihn gelesen? Haben sie schon den König
gesehen? Ich habe ihn noch nicht gesehen. Sie haben eine gute Feder;
leihen Sie sie nicht meiner Schwester. Da ist Ihr Bruder, sehen Sie
ihn? Wo sind Ihre Handschuhe? Leihen Sie sie Ihrer Tante. Wo
ist Ihr Regenschirm? Geben Sie ihn diesem Kinde. Meine Tante ist

tobt; kannten Sie sie? Was für Bücher haben Sie da? Haben Sie
sie gelesen? Wo ist dein Hund? Mein Vater hat ihn verkauft.

PAGE 34. No. 79.

Who has been here? Mr. Moll has been here; he has brought
this book. Hast thou been at the shoemaker's? I have been at
the shoemaker's to-day; he has already made your boots. Where
have you been this morning? We have been at our friend Charles',
who is very ill. This gentleman *was* three years in Vienna, and
his brother were a long time in Constantinople. Thou hast not
been industrious, thou hast not yet made thy exercise. I was
yesterday at Mrs. Rœder; she is a very amiable woman. Has Miss
N. been often in this town? She has already been here three times.
Did you know Mr. Scholl? I knew him in Berlin, we often walked
together. How long were you in Madrid? I was there only six
months, but I was nine months in Lisbon. Have you already seen
Messrs. Nollet? I saw them yesterday at the house of one of my
friends.

PAGE 35. No. 80.

Hat man meine Schuhe gebracht? Ja, man hat sie gebracht. Ist der
Schneider hier gewesen? Nein, er ist noch nicht hier gewesen. Bist du
bei dem Schreiner gewesen? Nein, ich bin noch nicht da gewesen. Wir
haben viele Blumen; wir sind im Garten des Herrn Nollet gewesen. Sind
Sie auch bei Herrn Moll gewesen? Mein Bruder ist nie zufriedener gewesen als heute. Er hat von seinem Onkel eine schöne goldene Uhr erhalten, und ein halbes Dutzend Schnupftücher. Wie lange sind Sie in
Paris gewesen? Wir sind sechs Monate da gewesen. Diese Herren haben viele Geschäfte gemacht; sie sind sehr glücklich gewesen. Sind die
Herren N. schon nach Köln abgereist? Sie sind heute Morgen mit ihrem
Herrn Onkel abgereist; ich habe sie bei Madame Sicard gesehen.

PAGE 35. No. 81.

Where wast thou this morning? I was at my cousin's, who has
arrived from Frankfort. My brother and I; we were at thy father's.
Your aunt had already left. Formerly Mr. Moll was very rich;
for the last ten years, he has lost much. Have you not yet been
at Mr. Mably's? I was there yesterday, but he was gone out. How
old was her brother, when he was in Cologne? He was ten or
eleven years old. We were not together; he was in Cologne and
I was in Dusseldorf. My sisters were a long time in Brussels, at
Mr. Nollet's. Why did you not come yesterday? I was ill yesterday. Were these gentlemen always so rich? Have they always
had as many friends? Have you been in school this morning? I
have not been in school to-day.

23

PAGE 35. No. 82.

Ich war ehemals viel glücklicher ; ich war jung und stark. Warst du immer so zufrieden als heute? Mein Vater war ehemals sehr reich. Sie waren ausgegangen, als ich kam. Wo waren Sie, als wir ankamen? Meine Schwestern waren gestern sehr krank. Wie alt waren Sie, als Sie zu N. waren? Ich war funfzehn Jahre und sechs Monate alt. War mein Zimmer offen, als Sie kamen (als Sie gekommen sind)? Nein, aber die Fenster waren offen. Dieses Mädchen war viel schöner, als sie jung war. Johann und Wilhelm waren immer meines Bruders Freunde. Waren Sie nicht bei meinem Bruder, als er sein Schnupftuch verloren hat?

PAGE 36. No. 83.

We had this week a visit from Messrs. Moll who have arrived with their sister. You had many friends when you were (still) young. We had more books than you. Our uncle had formerly many horses and many dogs. Thou wast very industrious, when thou hadst yet thy parents. These two merchants were formerly very rich; they had a large business. I had two brothers; the one was in Vienna, the other in Berlin. Hast thou known my two brothers? I have known the one who was in Berlin; the other was younger than I. Where is your cousin, who had so many birds? He has been in Brussels this year past. My penknife was lost; your brother has found it. Had you already written your letters, when we went out? We had not yet written them; we had no good pens and no good paper.

PAGE 36. No. 84.

Herr Maury war ehemals viel glücklicher, er hatte viele Freunde, viel Geld, viele Pferde und Hunde. Heinrich ist todt; er war ein guter Knabe, er hatte viel Verstand und Güte, er war von Jedermann geliebt. Wir waren oft in seinem Garten; seine Schwestern waren sehr liebenswürdig und sie hatten viele Blumen und Bücher. Seine Aeltern waren nicht reich, aber sie hatten ein großes Geschäft. Ich war gestern krank; ich hatte zu viel Obst gegessen. Hattest du deine Aufgaben noch nicht gemacht, als ich kam (als ich gekommen bin)? Nein, ich hatte sie noch nicht gemacht. Mein Bruder hatte schon die seinigen gemacht, als du kamst.

PAGE 36. No. 85.

Canst thou lend me this book? I cannot lend thee this book; it belongs to my cousin Henry. Who can read this letter? I can read it; it is very well written. We cannot write this morning. Why can you not write? We have no ink. Can you lend your watch to my brother? I cannot lend him my watch, I have sold it to Mr. S. Have you given my sister a pen? I have given her no pen. Have you a mind to buy this dog? I have no mind to buy him, he is not faithful. Has your brother nothing to do to-day? He has three letters to write. We have still two exercises to make. I had yesterday the pleasure of seeing your sister. Have you time to read this letter? I have no time now to read it. Can you give me an umbrella? I cannot give you one; I have only one. Your brother has the goodness to lend me his. Were you at my aunt's yesterday? No, I was not at her house yesterday; I had too much to do.

Page 37. No. 86.

Können Sie das thun? Ja, ich kann es; aber mein Bruder kann es nicht. Wollen Sie mir Ihr Federmesser leihen? Ich kann dir mein Federmesser nicht leihen; meine Schwester hat es genommen. Haben Sie meinem Vetter eine Feder gegeben? Ja, ich habe ihm eine gegeben. Hast du meiner Schwester deinen Hund verkauft? Ich habe ihr meinen Hund nicht verkauft. Kannst du deine Aufgabe nicht machen? Ich kann sie heute nicht machen. Wir können dieses Buch lesen. Diese Herren können ihre Briefe nicht schreiben; sie haben kein Papier. Hast du Lust, ein Paar Stiefeln zu kaufen? Hat dein Bruder Lust, seinen Ring zu verkaufen? Haben Sie die Güte gehabt, diesem armen Manne ein Glas Wasser zu geben? Mein Freund hat das Vergnügen gehabt, seine Aeltern zu sehen. Ich habe noch nicht Zeit gehabt, alle diese Briefe zu lesen. Mein Vater hat die Güte gehabt, mir eine goldene Uhr zu kaufen. Hast du sie (the watch) gesehen? Ich habe sie (the watch) noch nicht gesehen. Sind Sie heute bei Ferdinand gewesen? Ich war diesen Morgen bei ihm.

Page 37. No. 87.

Wilt thou go with me? I cannot go with thee, I have no time. I will lend thee a beautiful book, if thou art industrious. Can thy brother not come to-day? He has no mind to come; he is indisposed. We will now do our exercises. Will you drink a glass of wine? I have already drunk a glass of beer. I will eat a piece of meat or cheese. Do you wish a little mustard and salt? Can you lend us this (stick) cane? I cannot lend you this stick, my brother wants it. One cannot be more unhappy than this young man; he has lost his parents and his brothers and sisters. Who will have this apple? I will have it. What wilt thou do now? I will write a couple of letters. I will give you a basket of cherries, if you will be industrious. Will you have the goodness to give me a needle? I have none now, I cannot give you one. Have you time to go with us? I have no time to go with you. Have you already paid a visit to Messrs. N.? I have paid them a visit this morning.

25

PAGE 38. No. 88.

Was haſt du zu thun? Ich habe nichts zu thun. Willſt du dieſes Buch
leſen? Ja, ich will es leſen. Was macht (how is) dein Bruder? Er
iſt unwohl, er kann nicht kommen. Wo kann man dieſe ſchönen Feder⸗
meſſer kaufen? Man kann ſie bei dem Kaufmann kaufen, der bei un⸗
ſerm Nachbar wohnt. Wollen Sie mir ein wenig Dinte geben? Kann
Ihre Schweſter mir ihr Federmeſſer leihen? Was wollen dieſe Herren?
Dieſe Damen wollen einen Regenſchirm kaufen. Man kann nicht un⸗
glucklicher ſein, als ich bin; man kann nicht mehr Unglück haben als ich.
Geben Sie uns etwas zu trinken. Was wollen Sie haben? Wollen
Sie Wein oder Bier haben? Ich habe Ihnen meinen Stock geliehen.
Wo ſind Ihre Bruder? Ich habe ihnen meinen Hund verkauft. Dieſer
Mann iſt ſehr reich; alle dieſe Häuſer gehören ihm.

PAGE 38. No. 89.

The teacher has praised thee because thou hast been industrious.
Thy brother is a wicked boy; he has beaten me yesterday. Hast
thou already washed thyself? I have not yet washed myself; but
Henry has washed himself an hour ago. Why will thou beat my
dog? He has taken my bread. Our parents are best friends; we
will always love them. Charles, thou art very naughty; people
cannot love thee. How many glasses of wine hast thou drunk?
I have only drunk half a bottle of wine. Where hast thou been
this morning? I have been with my father at Mr. N's. Is Mr. N.
still indisposed? Since yesterday he has been a little better; but
he cannot yet eat nor drink. The physician has been with him
twice to-day. I will call upon him to-morrow also, or write him a
short letter. But why have you not yet been to see us (visited us).
I have not yet had time to visit you.

PAGE 39. No. 90.

Wer hat dich geſchlagen? Euer Vetter hat mich geſchlagen. Mit wem
willſt du dich ſchlagen? Ich will mich nicht ſchlagen. Ich habe keine Luſt
mich zu ſchlagen. Ludwig will ſich mit Heinrich ſchlagen. Die Magd hat
meine Hemden noch nicht gewaſchen. Sie will ſie jetzt waſchen. Ich
habe Ihnen mein Federmeſſer verkauft, aber Sie haben mir noch nicht
das Geld gegeben. Ihre Kinder ſind heute ſehr artig geweſen; der Leh⸗
rer hat ſie ſehr gelobt; er hat ihnen ein ſchönes Buch gegeben und einen
Korb Kirſchen. Warum hat der Lehrer uns noch nicht beſucht? Er hat
keine Zeit, er iſt immer in ſeiner Schule. Er iſt ein liebenswürdiger
Mann; er wird von allen ſeinen Schülern geliebt. Da iſt Ferdinand;
haſt du dich gewaſchen, mein Kind? Ja, Mama, ich habe mich ſchon ge⸗
waſchen.

PAGE 39. No. 91.

Can you tell me where Mr. Moll lives? I cannot tell you. Will you lend me this pen? I cannot lend it to you, it does not belong to me. I must pay a visit to-day to Miss S.; she has arrived yesterday with her mother. Must thou go already (now)? Where are my shoes? Has the shoemaker not yet brought them? No, he will send them to thee in an hour. How canst thou know that? He has told me so. I cannot believe it. Thy brother has still to make his exercises. We must do all our parents and teachers wish. You must (ought to) visit my cousin (once), he has been sick these three weeks. Henry and William must have many books. Who has given thee this ring? My aunt has given it to me. Louisa, I will tell thee something; thou hast a hole in thy stocking. I have already seen it, mother. Will you give my sister this thimble? I will give it to her now. Who has written you this letter? My cousin has written it to me.

PAGE 40. No. 92.

Mein Freund hat die Güte gehabt, mir einen Korb Kirschen zu senden. Sie haben mir noch nicht mein Buch geschickt. Ich habe noch nicht Zeit gehabt, es Ihnen zu senden. Wer hat meine Feder genommen? Ich kann es dir nicht sagen. Willst du mir nicht glauben? Dieses Federmesser gehört meinem Bruder; du mußt es ihm geben. Karl will mir seinen Regenschirm nicht leihen. Warum will er ihn dir nicht leihen? Mein Oheim ist angekommen. Euer Bruder hat es uns gesagt. Wer muß das thun? Ihre Schwestern müssen es thun. Sie müssen es Herrn Moll sagen. Dieser Brief ist nicht gut geschrieben; ich kann ihn nicht lesen. Hast du meinen Stock? Nein, ich habe ihn nicht. Ich habe ihn Ihnen geliehen. Sie haben ihn mir nicht geliehen.

———•———

PART III.

PAGE 40. No. 93.

What are you looking for? I am looking for my pen. My brother is looking for his pencil. We are looking for our dog. These children are looking for their books. Where do you buy your paper? We buy our paper at the booksellers. I do not find my cane. Who has taken my cane? I think your brother has taken it. I do not like this boy, he is always naughty. Thou lovest thy teacher. God loves the good (men). Good children love

their parents. Is it true that your uncle is selling his house? How
(dear) do you sell this cloth a yard? I sell this cloth at four dollars
a yard. That is very dear. Dost thou not find, Henry, that that
is very dear? Yes, I find it very dear. But we sell much of this
cloth. Everybody finds it beautiful. Send me three yards and a
half. Do you know where I live? Yes, you live in Peter-Street.
My servant can bring it to you to-day (yet).

PAGE 41. No. 94.

Was thun Sie? Ich lese das Buch, welches Ihr Bruder mir geliehen
hat. Sie lesen zu viel. Warum schreiben Sie nicht? Ich habe schon
drei Briefe geschrieben. Meine Vettern schreiben niemals. Sie tadeln
immer Ihre Vettern; man muß Niemand tadeln. Was machst du? Ich
mache meine Aufgaben. Was thut deine Schwester? Sie arbeitet. Was
trinken Sie? Ich trinke Wein und mein Bruder trinkt Bier. Wir trin=
ken keinen Wein. Ich esse Kirschen. Meine Brüder essen Pflaumen.
Sie essen immer, aber Sie arbeiten nicht. Können Sie mir sagen, wo
Herr N. wohnt? Er wohnt in der Wilhelmsstraße. Wohnst du bei dei=
nem Onkel? Nein, ich wohne nicht bei ihm. Gehst du nach Paris? Nein,
ich gehe nicht nach Paris. Ich liebe diesen jungen Mann nicht; er tadelt
immer seine Freunde. Er will mir nie sein Federmesser leihen. Ich leihe
ihm Alles, was ich habe. Wir leihen Alles unsern Freunden. Sie schlagen immer meinen Bruder; Sie sind sehr unartig. Diese Knaben schlagen
Jedermann. Verkaufen Sie Papier? Ich verkaufe Papier, Federn und
Dinte. Was sagen Sie? Ich sage, daß Sie mein Messer genommen
haben.

PAGE 41. No. 95.

Thy brother and I, we lived at N. in the same house. We were
together all day long. We made our exercises together; we played
together and had no greater pleasure than when we were together.
He loved me and I loved him so much that we were like brothers.
When thy father sent him something, we divided it (he shared it
with me). I often worked for him and he worked for me. The
teacher praised and loved us. All the good pupils were our friends;
they visited us every day; we told one another beautiful stories,
and laughed and danced till it was evening. You often sent us
handsome books, which gave us much pleasure. We had very
often time to read. When we had done our tasks, the teacher
always allowed us to play, or to read a useful book.

PAGE 42. No. 96.

Als wir jung waren, wohnten wir in diesem Hause. Ihre Schwester
kaufte einige Bänder und wählte das schönste für Sie. Ehemals liebte
ich das Spiel jetzt aber liebe ich Bücher. Dieses Volk liebte stets seinen

König. Dein Vetter suchte nach seinem Hut, als wir abreisten. Der Kaufmann, welchen du gestern suchtest, ist hier gewesen. Dein Bruder verkaufte sein Federmesser diesen Morgen. Während wir weinten, lachtet und tanztet ihr. Mein Vater erlaubte mir immer, gute Bücher zu lesen, und mit meinen Freunden zu spielen. Wir arbeiteten oft zusammen, als ihr bei eurem Oheim wohntet. Ich tanzte besser als Sie, aber Sie machten Ihre Aufgaben besser als ich. Du warst oft faul, und du hattest nicht immer Lust, zu lesen und zu schreiben. Ich erzählte dir schöne Geschichten, aber du liebtest das Spiel zu sehr, du spieltest den ganzen Tag. Der Lehrer tadelte dich oft, und die guten Schüler liebten dich nicht.

PAGE 42. No. 97.

This evening I shall have the pleasure of seeing my uncle. I shall give thee this handsome ring when thou (shalt be) art industrious. Henry will buy me to-day a handsome pair of gloves. Thy sister will be pleased, when she has made her exercise. When we shall be in N., we shall have much pleasure. When will you come to see me (visit me)? I think we shall call upon you to-morrow. My brothers will also come to-day or to-morrow. It will give my father a great deal of pleasure to see them once more. When will you write to your friend Charles? I shall write to him in a week or a fortnight. Will you have the goodness to send me the book, which you have promised me? I shall send it to you to-day, Miss. My servant will bring it to you. I had lent it to a friend, who has had it until now.

PAGE 43. No. 98.

Werdet ihr mit uns gehen? Ich glaube nicht, daß mein Vater es mir erlauben wird. Hat der Schuhmacher meine Stiefeln gebracht? Nein, er wird sie Ihnen diesen Abend bringen. Was werden wir jetzt thun? Wir werden ein Glas Wein trinken. Wollen Sie die Güte haben, mir Ihr Pferd zu leihen? Ich werde es Ihnen mit vielem Vergnügen leihen. Wir werden heute in dem Garten unsers Oheims spielen; er wird es uns erlauben. Ich werde Ihnen eine schöne Geschichte erzählen, wenn Sie gut und fleißig sind. Willst du heute arbeiten? Ich glaube, daß ich heute nicht arbeiten werde. Kommt hierher, meine Kinder; ihr werdet sehr müde sein. Wenn Ihre Vettern abgereist sind, so werden sie schönes Wetter haben. Deine Aufgabe ist schlecht gemacht; der Lehrer wir dich tadeln. Alle Schüler werden heute nach N. gehen. Karl, du mußt dich waschen, wenn du mit Heinrich gehen willst. Ja, Mama, ich werde mich jetzt waschen.

PAGE 43. No. 99.

I should be happier if I had books and friends. I should have more pleasure, if my cousin were here. Thou wouldst not be so rich, if thou hadst done less business. If Henry had money, he would buy these knives. I should visit thy brother, if I had time. Thou wouldst not love this dog so much, if he were not so faithful. We should not blame thee, if thou hadst been more industrious. Thy uncle told me, thou wouldst not come to-morrow. Which of these canes wouldst thou select? To whom would you give your flowers? What wouldst thou say, if I sold my dog? I should allow thee to play if thou hadst made thy exercise. These children would weep much, if their mother had departed. Thy father would tell us a fine story, if we had been better behaved. If thou hadst time I should lend thee a useful book. I would willingly go with you, but my teacher will not allow me (it); I have yet three letters to write to-day.

Page 44. No. 100.

Luiſe würde ſich ſehr freuen, wenn ſie alle dieſe Blumen hätte. Heinrich würde nicht ſo viele Freunde haben, wenn er nicht ſo gut und artig wäre. Wir würden noch nicht gekommen ſein, wenn wir nicht einen Brief von unſerm Vater erhalten hätten. Wir würden unſer Haus nicht verkauft haben, wenn mein Vater mehr Geſchäfte gemacht hätte. Der Lehrer würde dich tadeln, wenn du deine Aufgabe nicht gemacht hätteſt. Ich würde es nicht glauben, wenn du es nicht geſehen hätteſt. Wenn ich einen Apfel hätte, wir würden ihn theilen. Wir würden mit Ihnen gehen, wenn wir nicht ſo müde wären. Wenn ich Geld hätte, ſo würde ich ein Pfund Kirſchen kaufen. Wenn Sie mich liebten, ſo würde ich Sie auch lieben. Wenn Sie mir ſagten, wo Herr N. wohnt, ſo würde ich Ihnen ein Glas Wein geben. Würden Sie glauben, daß ich dies gethan habe? Würden Sie mir dieſen Gefallen thun, wenn ich Ihnen erlaubte, dieſen Abend zu ſpielen? Ich würde es gern thun, wenn ich Zeit hätte.

Page 44. No. 101.

I am not going out to-day; the weather is too bad. My brother will not go out either. If the weather were fine, we should like to go out. Henry thou never shuttest the door. Canst thou open this chest of drawers (bureau)? I close my room, when I go out. This evening I shall send you back the book which you have lent me. My cousin, yesterday, sent me back the cane which I had lent him. Dost thou copy all these letters? Must thou copy all that? I only copy as much as I please. I would copy this exercise again, if my teacher would allow me. I must communicate something to you. What do you want to communicate to me? I communicate to you some agreeable news. Why did you not communicate that to me earlier? What (dress) coat dost thou put on to-day? I put on my black dress, and my sister will put on her white dress. Where is the dress which you put on? Here it is.

Page 45. No. 102.

Stehen Sie noch nicht auf? Nein, ich bin unwohl, ich werde heute nicht aufstehen. Sie stehen immer sehr spät auf, das ist eine schlechte Gewohnheit. Ich gehe fort; ich habe viel zu thun. Ich werde auch fortgehen. Das Wetter ist so schön, daß ich Lust habe, einen Spaziergang zu machen. Machen Sie die Thür zu, wenn ich bitten darf. Oeffne das Fenster. Ihr Bruder öffnet immer die Thür und die Fenster. Gehen Sie nicht aus? Ich werde heute nicht ausgehen. Mein Vater will es nicht. Mein Bruder geht täglich zwei Mal aus. Ich werde Ihnen Ihren Regenschirm morgen zurücksenden. Senden Sie mir auch den Stock zurück, welchen ich Ihnen geliehen habe. Was thut mein Sohn? Er schreibt diese Briefe ab, welche Sie heute Morgen geschrieben haben. Mein Oheim ist angekommen; ich werde ihm die guten Nachrichten mittheilen. Ziehet euren neuen Anzug an; Herr N. besucht uns heute.

Page 45. No. 103.

This merchant is a cheat; he cheats everybody. We must cheat nobody. We cheat nobody. Thou always insultest me. Thy cousin yesterday insulted the whole company. Why do you insult this man? I received to-day a letter from my friend in Cologne. We receive every day news from our father. I shall receive money to-morrow. This mother brings up her children with much care. If we wish our children to become good, we should educate them with care. Charles, what art thou looking for? I have lost my ring. Thou art always losing something. Come, we must go, we cannot wait any longer; thou canst look for the ring afterwards. Go on, I shall come immediately; I shall find the ring. Why dost thou tear this paper? The paper is mine, I can tear it. I forbid thee to tear it. Wilt thou have the goodness to correct (me) my exercise? Thy brother always corrected my exercises, when he was (still) here. When are you going to give me back my pencil? Thy brothers never return what people lend them. Employ your time well. We should always make good use of our time.

Page 46. No. 104.

Ich will nicht länger warten. Ich verliere meine Zeit. Werden Sie heute spielen? Nein, wir werden nicht spielen, wir verlieren immer. Sie würden nicht verlieren, wenn Sie besser spielten. Wir würden besser spielen, wenn wir öfter spielten. Wenn ich mein Geld erhalte, werde ich noch ein Mal spielen. Verbietet Ihr Vater Ihnen nicht zu spielen? Ja, er verbietet es uns. Dieses Kind ist sehr unartig; es zerreißt seine Kleider. Mein Nachbar erzieht seine Kinder sehr schlecht. Ich liebe diesen jungen Mann nicht; er beleidigt mich immer. Heinrich verbessert seine Aufgabe; er wendet seine Zeit gut an. Derjenige, welcher sein Geld gut anwendet, ist weise. Wenn ihr mir meinen Bleistift zurückgebet, so werde ich euch eure Feder zurückgeben. Man muß immer zurückgeben, was man uns leiht.

PAGE 46. No. 105.

Have you already corrected your exercise? I have not yet corrected it, I shall correct it immediately. Your brother has offended me yesterday; I will have nothing more to do with him; from this day forward he is no longer my friend. We will take a walk together. I cannot go out this moment, I have already taken a walk this morning. Why have you not yet given me back my penknife? Who has opened the door? Who has communicated this news to you? Your father has told us yesterday a pretty story. My mother has given me permission to go this evening to N. Have you been at my cousin's yesterday? Yes, we have played, laughed and danced at his house all day long. But have you also worked? I do not think it, the teacher has already found fault with thee several times, thy sister has told me so often. Who has sent you this basket of cherries? Hast thou not yet called upon thy sick friend? My uncle has bought another horse; he has sold the old one to the coachman of our neighbor for twenty dollars.

PAGE 47. No. 106.

Du hast deine Zeit sehr schlecht angewendet, mein lieber Heinrich. Ich sehe, daß du nicht eine einzige Aufgabe gemacht hast. Ich habe dich immer gelobt, aber ich werde dich nicht mehr loben. Habt ihr zusammen gespielt, meine Kinder? Ja, Mama, wir haben gespielt und gearbeitet. Das ist sehr gut; ich werde euch Kirschen und Pflaumen geben. Ich werde sie vertheilen. Wir haben sie schon vertheilt. Warum haben Sie alle Fenster zugemacht? Das Wetter ist so schön; ich werde sie öffnen. Wer hat diese Briefe abgeschrieben? Ich glaube, daß Heinrich sie abgeschrieben hat. Haben Sie lange gewartet? Wir haben eine halbe Stunde gewartet. Herr N. hat den Regenschirm zurückgeschickt, welchen Sie ihm geliehen hatten. Ich habe von meiner Tante einen Brief erhalten, welchen ich noch nicht geöffnet habe. Ihr Vetter ist angekommen; er hat uns hundert Dinge erzählt. Man muß nicht Alles glauben, was er erzählt. Ich habe nicht Alles geglaubt.

PAGE 47. No. 107.

I come to tell thee that I start (depart) to-morrow. I have sent my servant to buy a pound of tobacco. We do not live in order to eat, but we eat in order to live. To be happy, we must be contented. To have friends, we should be kind (complacent). I have no time to go out. Have the goodness to copy these two letters. Will you be so good to open the door? We have a mind to take a short walk. My neighbor has two horses for sale. Who has permitted thee to go away so early? Is it not yet time to rise? I have had the pleasure of seeing Mr. Moll. Do you wish to speak to my father? I wish to speak to your mother. Have you money to buy this ring? Hast thou time to correct my exercise? Hast thy father given thee this money to make such bad use of it?

PAGE 47. No. 108.

Es ist kein Gegenstand, um zu lachen. Es ist sehr schwer. Ich habe das Vergnügen gehabt, mit Fräulein N. zu tanzen. Herr Nollet hat die Güte gehabt, mir sein Pferd zu leihen. Wünschen Sie mit mir auszugehen? Ich habe keine Zeit, nach N. zu gehen. Wir haben heute viel zu thun. Mein Bruder hat sechs Briefe abzuschreiben. Ich habe Ihnen gute Nachrichten mitzutheilen. Haben Sie die Güte, mir mein Buch zurückzusenden. Es ist Zeit abzureisen. Welches Kleid wünschen Sie anzuziehen. Erlauben Sie mir, das Fenster zu öffnen, es ist so warm. Ich bin gekommen, um zu sehen, ob sie wohl sind. Ich bin sehr unwohl, ich habe zu viel zu thun. Sie haben die schlechte Gewohnheit zu spät aufzustehen. Ein junger Mann muß früher aufstehen. Mein Freund hat das Unglück gehabt, seine Aeltern zu verlieren. Ich komme, um Ihnen Ihre Stiefeln zu bringen. Das ist sehr gut. Ich hatte keine Lust, länger zu warten.

PAGE 48. No. 109.

I am praised by my father, when I am industrious and well-behaved. Thou art found fault with (blamed) by thy teacher, because thou art always lazy. Henry is punished, because he is naughty. What man is praised and what man is blamed? The skilful man is praised, and the ignorant man is blamed. Which boys are rewarded, and which boys are punished? Those who are industrious are rewarded and those who are lazy are punished. We are loved by our parents, you are blamed by yours. My brothers are esteemed by everybody. We are despised by our enemies. Is this child never punished? By whom are you praised? Thy sister is blamed by her mother, because she does not work. I was always praised by my teacher, because I was industrious and well-behaved. Henry was always punished by his father, when he did not work.

PAGE 49. No. 110.

I have been punished by my father, because I have not copied these letters. Thou hast been rewarded by thy uncle, because thou hast found his watch. Henry has not been rewarded for his trouble. This news has been communicated to us by Mr. Moll. By whom has this exercise been corrected? We have been insulted several

33

times by this man. These gentlemen have been blamed much yesterday in the company. This child has been washed by its mother. I have been told (it has been told to me) that you are looking for a servant. By whom have these children been sent? These houses have all been sold yesterday. We have often been praised by our teacher, because we always did our exercises. Gustavus Adolphus has been (was) killed at Lutzen. The powder has been (was) invented by Berthold Schwarz. America has been (was) discovered by Columbus.

PAGE 49. No. 111.

Good day, dear Henry. I am glad to see thee again. How goes it? How art thou? I thank thee, I have been very well since I have been living in the country. How is thy brother? Is he well? Yes, he is very well. What art thou doing, Lewis? I am dressing myself. Are you not yet dressing yourselves? We shall dress later. Have you already washed yourself, Henrietta? I have not yet washed myself, but my sister has already washed herself. Is that my brother, who comes there with Mr. N.? You are mistaken (deceive yourself), it is not your brother. I do not think that I am mistaken. I am seldom mistaken. I have never been mistaken yet. We are going to N. this evening. I do not doubt, but we shall amuse ourselves well. How have you been amused yesterday at the concert? Very well, Mr. N. has played very well. I am astonished that you were not there. I had yet a great deal to do; I have worked till ten o'clock.

PAGE 50. No. 112.

Biſt du noch nicht angezogen, Karl? Ich werde mich jetzt anziehen. Warum haſt du dich noch nicht angezogen? Ich hatte noch zwei Aufgaben zu machen. Ich freue mich zu ſehen, daß du ſo fleißig biſt. Ich liebe Denjenigen, welcher ſich freut, wenn ſein Freund gelobt wird. Ich ſah Ihren Bruder geſtern. Sie irren ſich, mein Bruder iſt nicht mehr (longer) hier. Ich irre mich nicht, ich habe ihn mit ſeinem Freunde Ferdinand geſehen. Warum haben Sie ſich nicht gewaſchen? Ich würde mich gewaſchen haben, wenn ich Waſſer gehabt hätte. Wir waren geſtern auf dem Lande, wir haben uns ſehr unterhalten. Wie befindet ſich Ihre Schweſter? Sie iſt recht wohl, ſeit ſie bei ihrem Onkel geweſen iſt. Und wie haben Sie ſich befunden, ſeit ich Sie ſah? Ich bin ſehr wohl geweſen. Ich wundere mich, daß Sie noch nicht abgereiſt ſind. Ich werde heute Abend abreiſen.

PAGE 50. No. 113.

Is it raining? No, it is not raining. It was raining, when I came. It has rained all night. It will, certainly, rain to-morrow.

3

I think, it is snowing. Has it been snowing? If it snowed it would not rain. It will freeze to-night, for it is very cold. I must go out, but I see, it hails. I am very warm; it is lightning, it will thunder immediately. We will go home. I am glad, that I find you, but I am sorry that I cannot go with you. My uncle has arrived last night, and wishes us to dine with him to-day. Have you nothing to drink? I am very thirsty. Do you wish a glass of beer or a glass of water? You have only to say (command); here is what you wish. But I am also hungry, give me a piece of ham, and a little bread. You have fine pears and plums there. There is much fruit this year. Will you stay with us to-day? I thank you, I have promised my cousin to go to S. with him to-day; he certainly expects me already. Farewell.

Page 51. No. 114.

Was für Wetter ist es? Es ist schlechtes Wetter; es regnet. Es regnete nicht, als Sie kamen. Es wird den ganzen Tag regnen. Es hat diesen Morgen geregnet. Schneit es? Nein es schneit nicht. Es würde schneien, wenn es kälter wäre. Ich glaube, daß es friert. Das Wetter ist heute schöner; es ist warm. Ich bin sehr warm. Es hat geblitzt; es wird später donnern. Es thut mir leid, daß Sie nicht früher gekommen sind. Bist du hungrig? Ja ich bin hungrig und durstig. Ich habe einen langen Spaziergang gemacht. Ich werde ein Glas Wein trinken, wenn Sie es erlauben. Meine Schwester wird sich freuen, Sie wieder zu sehen. Sie hat oft mit mir von Ihnen gesprochen. Wird Ihr Neffe auch kommen? Ich zweifle, daß er kommen wird. Er hat zu viel zu thun.

Page 51. No. 115.

At what o'clock do you rise usually? I rise every morning at six o'clock, and go to bed at ten o'clock. Have you been for a walk? Yes; I have been walking in the woods for an hour. I am very tired, I will rest a little. What o'clock is it? It is eight o'clock; it is not yet half past eight o'clock. At what o'clock have you arrived? I have arrived a quarter past five. My sister has departed a quarter to eight. How long do you stay here? I shall only stay two or three days. At what o'clock do we dine? I think at twelve or half past one. At three o'clock we take our coffee, and at seven o'clock we take supper. The Germans eat four times every day, and the French only twice. I find, that the French are right. Man does not live to eat and to drink.

Page 51. No. 116.

Haben Sie die Güte, mir zu sagen, wieviel Uhr es ist. Es ist noch nicht elf Uhr, es ist halb zehn. Ich muß um zwölf Uhr oder um halb eins fortgehen. Haben Sie schon zu Mittag gegessen? Nein, ich werde mit meinem Vetter zu Mittag essen; wir speisen gewöhnlich um zwei Uhr. Um wieviel Uhr essen Sie zu Abend? Ich werde um neun Uhr zu Abend essen. Haben Sie Lust, ein wenig spazieren zu gehen? Wenn es nicht regnet, will ich ein wenig mit Ihnen spazieren gehen. Es ist schönes Wetter; wir wollen nach N. gehen; wir werden dort eine zahlreiche Gesellschaft finden. Sind Sie schon müde? Ich bin sehr müde; es ist zu warm. Wenn Sie erlauben, will ich ein wenig ausruhen. Stehen Sie auf, es ist Zeit, nach Hause zu gehen. Ich muß vor zehn Uhr zu Bette gehen, um morgen früh um fünf Uhr aufstehen zu können.

PAGE 52. No. 117.

For whom are these books? This one is for me and that one is for my sister. Where is the young man, for whom you have bought all these things? Through what street must we go to get to the market? Through Frederic-Street or William-Street. Do you go out without an umbrella? It will rain immediately. What is life without a friend? I cannot live without thee. Thou hast gone out against the will of thy father. Why is thy brother always against me? Where dost thou come from? I come from a walk, from school, from church. The maid-servant is coming from the cellar, out of the garden, out of the kitchen. With whom did you go out? With the uncle, with the aunt, with you. After dinner, we are going out. When are you coming back? Will you come back before us or after us? We shall return after you. Where is my sister? She is in the church, in the garden, in the market. Where is thy mother going? She is going to the kitchen, to the cellar, to the market. Where hast thou put my book? I have put it on the table, under the chair. Where is little Louisa? She is sitting on the chair, under the table, at the door. Are you writing to your cousin or to your female cousin? Of whom are you thinking? I am thinking of the poor woman whom I saw at your house yesterday.

PAGE 52. No. 118.

Dieses ist für mich; Jenes ist für Sie. Derjenige, welcher nicht für mich ist, ist gegen mich. Ich kann dieses nicht ohne ihn, ohne sie, ohne euch, thun. Ich werde vor Ihnen ankommen; Sie werden nach mir ankommen. Sie sind undankbar gegen uns. Ich denke immer an Sie, aber Sie denken niemals an mich. Da ist deine kleine Schwester; hast du nichts für sie? Ihr liebt meinen Bruder nicht; ihr seid immer gegen ihn. Wo ist Ihr Sohn? Dieses Obst und diese Blumen sind für ihn. Wo sind Sie gewesen? Wir sind in der Kirche und in der Schule gewesen. Wohin gehen Sie? Wir gehen in den Garten, auf den Markt, in die

Küche. Woher kommen dieſe Kinder? Sie kommen von dem Spazier=
gange, von (aus) der Kirche, von (aus) dem Garten. Wo haben Sie
meine Strümpfe und Schuhe hingelegt? Ich habe ſie auf Ihren Stuhl,
auf den Tiſch, in den Schrank gelegt. Haben Sie meinen Bruder geſehen?
Ich habe ihn auf dem Spaziergange, in dem Garten, an der Thür, ge=
ſehen. Ich ſchreibe an meinen Oheim und an meine Tante. Wir ſprechen
oft von ihm und von ihr.

PAGE 53. No. 119.

The servant-maid is in the cellar or in the garden. We are going
this evening to the theatre or to the concert. Are you sending the
servant to the shoemaker or to the tailor? Shall we go to our
aunt to-day or shall we stay at home? Were you yesterday at the
minister's? Do you come to (see) me or to (see) my brother? Why
do you always sit near the fire? Are you so cold? What is the
matter with your eye, with your foot? Why do you wear a feather
in your hat? Place yourself near the door or near the window.
Have you received this flower from the gardener? You work from
morning till night. What are you doing under the table? I am
looking for my pencil. Charles has put it into the writing-stand.

PAGE 54. No. 120.

What are you speaking of? Is this the book, you are speaking
of? What have you done that with? Is that the pen, with which
you have written this letter? What are you using that for? (what
use do you make of that?) What are you thinking of then? Is
that the house in which your uncle lives, the town through which
you have passed? Have people talked of my misfortune? Yes,
they have spoken of it. Have you thought of my business? No,
I have not thought of it. Are you satisfied with your new piano?
No, I am not satisfied with it. Is there any more wine in the
bottle? No, there is no more in it. How many yards do you
require for a new coat? I require three yards and a half. Come
up. Go down. Why do you not come in? Why do you not go
in? The boy went too near the water and fell in. Will you go to
the theatre this evening? We shall not go, but Henry and Charles
are going.

PAGE 54. No. 121.

Wiſſen Sie, wovon ich ſpreche, woran ich denke? Das iſt nicht dieſelbe
Straße, wodurch wir dieſen Morgen gekommen ſind, daſſelbe Haus, wo
wir geſtern geweſen ſind. Sprechen Sie vom Kriege? Ja, wir ſprechen
davon. Denken Sie ans Concert? Wir denken nicht daran. Sind Sie
mit dieſem Ringe zufrieden? Ich bin ſehr damit zufrieden. Warum kom=
men Sie nicht herauf? Sagen Sie Ihrem Bruder, daß ich ſogleich hin=

unter kommen werde. Kommen Sie herein, meine Freunde. Ich bitte Sie, herein zu kommen. Gehen Sie diesen Abend ins Schauspiel? Wir werden nicht hingehen. Wissen Sie, wo dieser Herr wohnt, wo er hingeht, und wo er ist? Wir wissen es nicht.

PAGE 54.   No. 122.

Amelia has lost her little hat. We have planted three pretty little trees. To whom belongs this pretty little garden? How much hast thou paid for this little pigeon? Where are these little gentlemen going to? Come, Louisa, we will go to my aunt, she has another little cat and a little dog. I have just received a little letter from my sister, wherein she requests me to buy her a little knife and a little spoon. I will be very good, my dear mother, if you will buy me a new little dress. Carry these little tables into the garden, Henrietta, we will work there a short hour. What little village do I see there below in the forest? What child has lost these little shoes? Frederic has obtained a pretty little bird from the gardener. To whom belong all these little flowers? Where is thy little sister, John?

PAGE 55.   No. 123.

Henry, hast thou a mind to take a walk with me? I have no mind to go out now. I am sleepy. Art thou not ashamed, to be so lazy? Come, we will go to the garden of my uncle. What o'clock is it? It is only six o'clock, the sun is still shining (is still high). Thou are right, it is yet early, I will go with thee. I am in the habit of going for a walk every evening, before I go to bed. That is a good habit. But I am very warm; we are walking too fast. I am very thirsty, I should like to drink. When we are warm, we ought not to drink. I require to rest a little; I am so tired that I can go no further. Thou must have a moment's patience. Come, I fear to get home too late.

PAGE 55.   No. 124.

Wie, sind Sie noch im Bett? Schämen Sie sich nicht, so lange zu schlafen? Ich würde mich schämen, so spät aufzustehen. Ich kann heute nicht aufstehen, ich habe Kopfweh. Sie sind ein kleiner Faulenzer. Wenn Sie in die Schule gehen müssen, so sehen Sie sich immer nach einem Vorwande um. Sie pflegen früh zu Bett zu gehen und spät aufzustehen. Das ist eine schlechte Gewohnheit. Ich bitte Sie, einen Augenblick Geduld zu haben. Ich werde sogleich aufstehen. Ich habe keine Lust, länger zu warten. Ich fürchte, zu spät zur Kirche zu kommen. Sie sind sehr hartherzig; Sie haben kein Mitleid für einen armen Kranken. Sie sind nicht krank; Sie haben keine Lust in die Schule zu gehen. Sie haben

Recht, mein Freund, ich werde mich bemühen, diesen Fehler abzulegen und Ihrem guten Rathe zu folgen.

PAGE 56. No. 125.

Ich glaube, daß es schon spät ist. Wir glauben es nicht. Auch glaubt es mein Bruder nicht. Glauben Sie es? Ich glaube es nicht. Wenn ich es glaubte, würden Sie lachen. Ich habe dies nie geglaubt. Wer würde das geglaubt haben? Ich würde es glauben, wenn Sie es mir sagten. Es ist eine unglaubliche Sache. Sie würden es wol glauben, wenn Sie es sähen. Diese Herren glauben es nicht. Wie sollte ich das glauben? Ihr Bruder glaubte Alles, was man ihm sagte; er war zu leichtgläubig. Er würde es nicht glauben, wenn er sie kennte.

PAGE 56. No. 126.

Ich habe Ihnen etwas zu sagen. Was haben Sie mir zu sagen? Ich sage Ihnen nichts. Sagen Sie es nur mir. Ich werde es Ihnen ein ander mal sagen. Sie werden meinem Bruder nicht sagen, was ich Ihnen geschrieben habe. Sagen Sie ihm nicht, daß ich noch im Bette bin. Was hat er Ihnen gesagt? Habe ich es Ihnen nicht gesagt? Sie haben es mir noch nicht gesagt. Wollen Sie, daß ich es sage? Man muß nicht Alles sagen, was man weiß. Er hat es mir ins Ohr gesagt. Ihr Oheim sagte mir gestern, daß er sein Haus verkaufen würde. Was sagen Sie dazu? Ich würde es Ihnen mit Vergnügen sagen, wenn ich es wüßte. Wenn ich anders sagte, würde ich lügen.

PAGE 56. No. 127.

Ich wünsche, daß Ihr Unternehmen gelingen möge. Wir wünschen oftmals Sachen, die uns schädlich sind. Ich würde wünschen, Ihnen dienen zu können. Ich hoffe, daß unser Freund die Stelle erhalten wird, welche er wünscht. Sie hoffte, ihren Proceß zu gewinnen, aber sie täuschte sich. Mein Vetter hat nichts mehr zu hoffen. Wir hoffen Alles von der Vorsehung. Meine Schwester hofft, daß Sie thun werden, was Sie ihr versprochen haben. Wünsche nie, was du nicht haben kannst. Was wünschen Sie? Worauf hoffen Sie? Ich glaube, daß mein Vater heute ankommen wird. Wir müssen es hoffen. Diese Herren wünschten, daß wir abreisten. Wünscht Ihre Schwester mit uns zu gehen?

PAGE 57. No. 128.

Ich schreibe einen Brief an meinen Bruder. Meine Mutter wird ihm morgen schreiben. Sie schrieben früher besser. Was haben Sie ihm geschrieben? Haben Sie noch nicht an ihn geschrieben, daß unser Freund Heinrich todt ist? Schreiben Sie ihm das. Wenn ich eine gute Feder hätte, würde ich auch schreiben. Sie schreiben zu schnell; schreiben Sie langsamer. Zeigen Sie mir, was Sie geschrieben haben. Sie müssen noch einmal schreiben. Was lesen Sie? Ich lese ein unterhaltendes Buch. Was lasest du gestern, als du bei deinem Onkel warst? Ich las

Gellert's Fabeln, welche sehr gut geschrieben sind. Wir würden öfter lesen, wenn wir mehr Zeit hätten. Wie muß man dieses Wort lesen? Erinnert euch wohl, was ihr gelesen habt. Wollen Sie, daß ich Ihnen diesen Brief lesen soll? Ich möchte wohl wie Sie lesen können.

PAGE 57. No. 129.

Was sehe ich? Sehen Sie es nicht? Ich sehe nichts. Aber sehen Sie doch ein mal. Es ist wohl der Mühe werth es zu sehen. Ich sah Ihren Vetter gestern. Haben Sie. ihn nicht gesehen? Sehen Sie, wie ich dies mache? Ihr Vetter sieht mich nicht. Wenn ich meinen Freund sähe (see), würde ich ihm sagen, daß Sie hier sind. Wollen Sie, daß ich ein Licht bringe; oder können Sie noch sehen? Ich habe Herrn N. heute gesehen. Kennt er mich? Ich glaube, daß er Sie kennt. Er hat mich gegrüßt. Haben Sie auch meinen Onkel gekannt? Haben Sie mir nicht gesagt, daß Sie ihn kennen? Ich würde ihn wieder erkennen, wenn ich ihn sähe. Ihr Bruder hat mich an meiner Stimme wieder erkannt. Diese Kinder erkennen mich nicht wieder.

PAGE 58. No. 130.

Wo gehen Sie hin? Ich gehe zu meiner Tante, und mein Bruder geht zur Schule. Wo gingen Sie diesen Morgen mit Ihrem Vetter hin? Wir gingen in die Kirche. Ich würde gern spazieren gehen, wenn Sie mit mir gehen würden. Ich werde mit Ihnen gehen, aber gehen Sie nicht so schnell. Wo ist Ihre Schwester? Sie ist zu ihrem Onkel gegangen. Wir würden zusammen gegangen sein, wenn ich Zeit gehabt hätte. Werden Sie morgen nicht nach N. gehen? Mein Vater will nicht, daß ich dahin ginge. Ich gehe weg. Gehen Sie schon weg? Heinrich geht noch nicht weg. Wilhelm ist schon weggegangen. Gehen Sie weg. Ich muß weggehen. Ich glaube, daß Ihre Freunde schon weggegangen sind. Um welche Zeit gehen Sie aus? Ich gehe jeden Morgen um sieben Uhr aus. Und um welche Zeit gehst du aus? Ich ging gestern um sechs Uhr aus. Ist Ihr Bruder schon ausgegangen? Morgen werde ich früh ausgehen. Ich muß um halb zwei ausgehen. Meine Mutter wollte nicht, daß ich ausginge.

PAGE 58. No. 131.

Woher kommen Sie so spät? Wir kommen aus dem Garten. Elise kommt heute nicht. Sie ist mit ihrem Vater auf das Land gegangen. Kommen Sie diesen Nachmittag zu mir. Es ist möglich, daß ich komme. Ich wünschte, daß Sie früh kämen. Früher kamen Sie alle Tage. Ich würde öfter kommen, wenn ich nicht so viel zu thun hätte. Mein Bruder ist noch nicht zurückgekommen. Er will diesen Abend zurückkommen. Mein Onkel kommt nicht mehr zurück. Wir sahen Ihren Onkel, als wir vom Lande zurückkamen. Um welche Zeit kommt die Post an? Ich glaube, sie (die Post) kommt um drei Uhr an. Gestern kam sie (die Post) ser spät. Früher kam sie um zwei Uhr an. Meine Schwestern werden heute von Lüttich ankommen.

40

PAGE 58. No. 132.

Haben Sie nichts zu trinken? Ich trinke keinen Wein. Wir trinken nur Wasser, und mein Bruder trinkt Bier. Sie trinken nicht. Ich habe die Ehre auf Ihre Gesundheit zu trinken. Als ich jung war, trank ich nichts als Milch. Dieser Herr hat ein wenig zu viel getrunken. Er ißt nicht viel, aber er trinkt viel. Wer hat aus meinem Glase getrunken? Ich will nicht mehr trinken. Wir wollen noch ein Glas trinken. Der Wein, welchen wir gestern tranken, war so gut, daß Jeder eine Flasche trank. Trinken Sie Ihr Glas aus. Sie haben Ihr Glas noch nicht ausgetrunken. Trinken Sie noch einmal. Haben Sie keinen Appetit? Essen Sie ein wenig Schinken. Ich habe genug gegessen, ich habe keinen Appetit mehr. Sie werden noch ein Stück Fleisch essen. Dieses Kind ißt den ganzen Tag. Wir aßen vor einigen Tagen köstliche Fische. Um welche Zeit aßen wir zu Mittag? Ich esse gewöhnlich um zwei Uhr zu Mittg, aber heute esse ich um vier Uhr zu Mittag. Nach dem Mittagsessen trinke ich eine Tasse Kaffee und dann gehe ich spazieren.

PAGE 59. No. 133.

Können Sie mir sagen, was die Uhr ist? Ich kann es Ihnen nicht sagen, ich habe meine Uhr nicht bei mir. Wenn ich sie bei mir hätte, könnte ich es Ihnen genau sagen. Ich werde heute nicht ausgehen können; mein Vater ist krank. Mein Bruder wird nicht kommen können. Ich wollte jedoch, daß er kommen könnte. Ich würde Ihnen dieses Buch leihen können, wenn es mir gehörte. Ludwig kann diesen Brief auf die Post tragen. Ich konnte gestern nicht ausgehen. Mein Freund konnte auf Ihren Brief nicht antworten, weil er zu viel zu thun hatte. Wissen Sie, wann mein Vater zurückkommen wird? Ich weiß nicht. Weiß es Ihre Schwester? Wir wissen Alle, daß wir sterben müssen. Können Sie tanzen? Ich habe es gekonnt, aber ich kann es nicht mehr. Mein Vater konnte mehrere Sprachen. Heinrich kann deutsch sprechen. Diese Knaben können weder lesen noch schreiben. Die Männer wissen nicht, ihre Zeit anzuwenden. Ich wußte nicht, daß Ihr Bruder abgereist war. Ich werde bald wissen, wer dies gethan hat. Wie können Sie glauben, daß ich dies wüßte? Ich wollte, daß Sie es wüßten.

PAGE 59. No. 134.

Was thun Sie? Ich thue, was Sie mir befohlen haben. Was thaten Sie, als ich herein kam? Ich zündete das Feuer an. Was wollen Sie diesen Abend thun? Ich werde diesen Abend nichts thun. Ihr Bruder thut nichts als laufen. Diese Kinder thun nichts als essen und trinken. Wenn man seine Pflicht gethan hat, hat man sich nichts vorzuwerfen. Sie haben eine gute Handlung gethan. Warum sind Sie übler Laune? Was haben Sie Ihnen gethan? Man muß den Willen Gottes thun. Sie wollen ihm schreiben; an Ihrer Stelle würde ich es nicht thun. Ich werde mein Möglichstes thun, ihn zu befriedigen. Ich nehme dieses für mich. Wie viele Bücher nehmen Sie? Ihr Bruder nimmt immer meine

Feder. Wollen Sie meinen Platz nehmen? Nimm, was du willst. Nimm dieses Kind bei der Hand. Wer hat mein Schreibebuch genommen? Ihr Vetter nahm gestern meinen Stock. Ich werde einen dieser Aepfel nehmen, wenn Sie es erlauben. Ich habe mir die Freiheit genommen, ihm zu schreiben. Wir nahmen einige Stühle, und wir setzten uns. Wenn ich diese Bücher nähme, würde mein Vater mit mir schmälen.

Page 60. No. 135.

Wir schlafen zu viel; Sie schlafen weniger als wir. Ich schlafe gewöhnlich sieben Stunden. Ehedem schlief ich länger. Mein Bruder schlief gestern bis acht Uhr; aber morgen wird er nicht so lange schlafen, weil er um vier Uhr nach Köln abreisen muß. Unsere Mutter erlaubt uns nicht länger, als bis sechs Uhr zu schlafen. Ich schlafe sehr fest. Sie schliefen gestern sehr unruhig. Dieses Kind schläft sehr sanft. Wir haben kein Messer, unser Brod zu schneiden, deshalb brechen wir es. Sie werden diesen Stock brechen, wenn Sie ihn beugen. Ich glaube nicht, daß er bricht. Ich möchte nicht, daß er bräche. Dieser Knabe hat eine Scheibe zerbrochen. Er zerbrach zwei in letzter Woche. Diese Magd ist sehr unbedachtsam; sie zerbricht jeden Tag etwas. Gestern zerbrach sie zwei Gläser, und am Sonntag ein halbes Dutzend Tassen.

Page 61. No. 136.

Ich weiß nicht, wozu ich mich entschließen soll; was rathen Sie mir zu thun? Der Eine räth mir dieses, der Andere jenes. Man rieth mir gestern, einen Theil meiner Rechte abzutreten. Ich wollte, daß Sie mir riethen; ich habe zu Ihnen das meiste Zutrauen. Da Sie wünschen, daß ich Ihnen rathe, sage ich Ihnen, daß der magerste Vergleich besser ist als der fetteste Proceß. Ich werde Ihnen die Früchte bringen, welche Sie wünschen. Ich glaube, Sie haben Sie mir schon gebracht. Man brachte mir gestern einige Briefe aus Berlin. Wenn Sie zurückkommen, bringen Sie Ihre Schwester mit. Herr N. will seinen Sohn morgen mitbringen. Sie brachten Ihre Tante von Wien mit. Ich wünsche, Sie brächten den jungen Mann mit, von welchem Sie gesprochen haben. Er empfiehlt mir seinen Sohn. Sie empfahlen ihm ihr Geschäft. Ich habe ihm empfohlen, über ihn zu wachen.

⎯⎯◆⎯⎯

Page 61.

EXERCISES FOR READING AND TRANSLATING.

1. THE LITTLE DOG.

A young lady, named Caroline, was one day walking on the banks of a river. Here she met some bad boys, who wanted to drown a little dog; she took compassion upon the poor animal, bought it and took it with her to the castle.

The little dog soon had made the acquaintance of his new mistress, and did not leave her a moment. One evening, when she was going to bed, the little dog suddenly began to bark. Caroline took the candle, looked under the bed and perceived a frightful looking man, who had concealed himself there. It was a thief.

Caroline called for help, and all the inhabitants of the castle hastened to her, when they heard her cry. They seized the robber and handed him over to justice. When interrogated (on his trial) he confessed, that it had been his intention to murder the young lady, and rob the castle.

Caroline thanked Heaven for having preserved her so wonderfully, and said: "Nobody would have believed, that the little animal, whose life I saved, would have saved mine!"

PAGE 62.

2. THE GOOD NEIGHBORS.

The little boy of a miller approached too near a brook, and fell in. The smith, who lived on the other side of the brook, saw it, jumped into the water and pulled out the child, and brought it to its father.

A year after a fire broke out in the shop of the smith during the night. The house was completely in flames, before the smith observed it. He saved himself with his wife and children; only his youngest daughter had been forgotten in the first terror.

The child commenced to cry in the burning house, but no one would venture in, when suddenly the miller appeared, rushed into the flames, safely brought the child out, and placed it in the arms of the smith, saying:

"God be praised for having given me an opportunity of showing you my gratitude. You have taken my son out of the water, and I, with the help of God, have saved your daughter from the flames"

PAGE 63.

3. THE BROKEN HORSE-SHOE.

A farmer was going to town with his son, little Thomas. "Look," said he on the way, "there lies a piece of a horse-shoe on the ground: take it up and put it into your pocket." "Pshaw," replied Thomas, "it is not worth while stooping for." The father said nothing, took the horse-shoe and put it into his pocket. In the next village he sold it to a blacksmith for three cents, and bought cherries for them.

After this they continued their way. The sun was burning hot. No house, nor wood, nor spring was to be seen far or near. Thomas was dying with his thirst, and could only follow his father with difficulty.

Then the latter, as if by accident, dropped a cherry. Thomas took it up as greedily, as if it were gold; and quickly put it into his mouth. A few steps further the father dropped another cherry, which Thomas seized with the same greediness. This continued until he had picked them all up.

When he had eaten the last one, the father turned to him, and said: "Look, if you had been inclined to stoop once for the horse-shoe, you need not have done so a hundred times for the cherries."

PAGE 63.

4. THE HIDDEN TREASURE.

Shortly before his death, a farmer said to his three sons: "Dear children, I can bequeath nothing to you but this hut, and the vine-yard which adjoins it. But in this vineyard lies a treasure. Dig diligently, and you will find it."

After the death of the father, the sons dug up the vineyard with the greatest assiduity, yet found neither gold nor silver. But as they had never cultivated the soil with so much care before, it produced so large a quantity of grapes, that they were astonished at it.

Now, the sons found out what their father had meant by the treasure, and they wrote over the door of the vineyard, in large characters: "Industry is the greatest treasure of man."

PAGE 64.

5. THE OAK AND THE WILLOW.

After a very stormy night, a father went with his son into the field, to see what damage the storm had caused. "Do look!" exclaimed the boy, "there lies the big, strong oak, stretched on the ground, whilst the weak willow near the brook stands still quite upright. I should have thought that the storm would have sooner blown down the willow than the oak."

"My son," said the father, "the proud oak, which could not bend, was forced to break; but the pliable willow yielded to the storm, and was therefore spared."

6. THE GRATEFUL LION.

A poor slave, who had escaped from the house of his master, was condemned to death. He was conducted into a large square, surrounded by walls, where they let loose against him a formidable lion. Thousands of people witnessed this spectacle.

The lion made a furious spring at the man; but, suddenly, he stopped, wagged his tail, jumped around him with joy, and in a friendly manner, licked his hands. Everybody was astonished, and asked the slave, what this meant.

The slave related: "When I had escaped from my master, I concealed myself in a cave, in the midst of the wilderness; when, suddenly this lion came in, whined and showed me his paw, in which stuck a large thorn. I drew out the thorn, and from that time the lion supplied me with game, and we lived peacefully together in the hut. At the last chase, we were taken and separated from one another. Now the good beast rejoices to have found me again."

Everybody was delighted at the gratitude of this wild beast, and loudly demanded the pardon of the slave and of the lion. The slave obtained his freedom and many rich gifts. The lion followed him like a little dog, and always remained with him, without hurting anybody.

SECOND COURSE.

PAGE 72. No. 1.

The rose is a beautiful flower. John is an idle boy. Louisa is an industrious girl. Our grandmother is an old woman. The dog is a useful animal. This poor man is very sick. Last night was a very cold night. Henry is my old friend. Theresa is my youngest sister. The count has a blind son and a blind daughter. Your neighbor possesses a handsome house and a large garden.

PAGE 72. No. 2.

Sie haben eine schlechte Feder. Heinrich hat einen guten Vater und eine gute Mutter. Wir haben einen treuen Bedienten. Unser Nachbar bewohnt ein sehr kleines Haus. Diese Blume hat einen angenehmen Geruch. Wir lernen die deutsche Sprache. Mein Sohn hat ein französisches Buch gelesen. Mein Onkel hat einen englischen Brief erhalten. Meine Schwester hat ihre schwarze Katze verloren. Ludwig hat seinen kleinen Hund wiedergefunden. Die Magd hat ein gutes Feuer gemacht.

PAGE 72. No. 3.

My brother drinks no beer and no wine. To-day we eat no soup and no meat. Have we no bread and no sugar? I eat no black (rye) bread. This gentleman is not a Frenchman. This lady is not an Englishwoman. My uncle has no children. I have no mind to go walking. I have no money about me. My brother too has not a penny. My sons have no (longer any) more pigeons. Charles has no longer a friend. We read no more German books. I am no longer a child. I do not speak German, or I am not speaking German.

PAGE 73. No. 4.

Ich habe keine Feder und keine Tinte. Mein Vetter hat keine Handschuhe. Die Vögel haben keine Zähne. Dieser Knabe ißt kein Obst. Diese Frau trinkt kein Bier. Dieser Herr spricht kein Englisch. Was trinken Sie? Wir trinken gutes Bier und guten Wein. Ich habe keine Tinte und kein Papier mehr. Dieses junge Mädchen hat schöne Zähne. Diese arme Mutter hat keine Kinder mehr. Dieser Mann ist kein Schuhmacher. Mein Sohn liest keine englischen Werke mehr.

(45)

PAGE 73. No. 5.

Where is thy brother? I believe he is in the garden or in the kitchen. Have you been in school to-day? My sister has been in the country these three days; she is not well. Where are you going now? I am going to church with my brother, and from there we shall go to the exchange. Take this letter to the post-office, before you go to the theatre. Where have you put my pen-knife? I have put it into the drawer. Where do these boys come from? I believe they come from the forest. When Charles comes from school, send him to me, I will make him a present of a hand-some book.

PAGE 73. No. 6.

Wo seid ihr gewesen, meine Kinder? Wir sind in der Schule und in der Kirche gewesen. Ist der Kutscher in dem Stalle? Ist die Magd in dem Keller? Meine Mutter ist auf dem Markt gewesen, und mein Vater auf der Post. Wir werden heute Abend auf den Ball gehen. Meine Brüder werden in das Concert oder in das Schauspiel gehen. Meine Neffen sind seit zwei Monaten auf dem Lande. Dieser Mann geht alle Tage ins Wirthshaus. Wo kommen Sie jetzt her? Wir kommen von einem Spaziergange. Meine Tante kommt von der Kirche, und mein Onkel kommt von der Börse. Ihr Neffe kommt aus dem Garten. Legen Sie diese Tellertücher in die Schublade und dieses Tischtuch in den Schrank. Gehen Sie nicht aus dem Zimmer.

PAGE 73. No. 7.

Have you had any pleasure in the country? Have you any relations in Cologne? We have no relations there, but many friends. My neighbor has money and credit, and yet he is not satisfied. This young man has much intelligence and much knowledge; he is very modest. I have had bad luck; I have done a bad business. Your children possess industry and modesty; they are loved and praised by everybody. My uncle owns large estates, splendid palaces and magnificent gardens. In our country there are large towns, handsome villages, rich merchants, industrious peasants and excellent wine.

PAGE 74. No. 8.

Sie haben heute gespielt; haben Sie Glück gehabt? Wir haben Unglück gehabt; wir haben Alles verloren. Wenn wir Geld hätten, würden wir auch Freunde haben. Wenn Sie Verdruß hätten, würden Sie nicht so munter sein. Wir würden Vergnügen gehabt haben, wenn Sie bei uns gewesen wären. Es ist möglich, daß Sie Kenntnisse haben, aber Sie sind nicht bescheiden. Wenn dieser Mann Glück gehabt hätte, würde er nicht so arm sein. Es ist traurig, Feinde zu haben, die uns verfolgen.

PAGE 74. No. 9.

Henry has lost his golden watch. Louisa has broken her silver spoon. Silk stuffs are dearer than cotton ones. This knife has a wooden handle. We have seen a stone bridge and a marble staircase. Give me my thread stockings and my leather shoes. Tobacco keeps best in a leaden box. Have you read yesterday's paper? That of to-day has not yet arrived. My sister has an ivory thimble. My father has bought thirty yards of Silesia linen. The Austrian Emperor is beloved by his people. The Russian ambassador has departed.

PAGE 75. No. 10.

Ich liebe die wollenen Strümpfe nicht; ich ziehe baumwollene vor. Dieser Saal ist mit marmornen Bildsäulen geschmückt. Mein Onkel hat mir eine goldene Kette gegeben. Ich bin müde; ich will mich ein wenig auf dieser steinernen Bank ausruhen. Ziehen Sie seidene oder metallene Knöpfe vor? Eisernes Werkzeug ist dauerhafter als hölzernes. Unsere Magd hat zwei silberne Löffel verloren. Das heutige Schauspiel gefällt mir mehr als das gestrige. Der morgende Ball wird sehr herrlich sein. Wir lieben die französischen Weine und die holländischen Käse. Der spanische Gesandte ist stolzer als der englische.

PAGE 75. No. 11.

Who is this gentleman? Who is this lady? Who has given you this ring? To whom have you lent your umbrella? From whom have you received this handsome pocket-book? Whom are you looking for? For whom is this handsome watch? Whose child is sick? Whose book is this? Which of these canes is yours? Which of these pens is the best? Which of these children is your nephew. From which of these officers have you bought the horse? What have you paid for it? Of what is your brother speaking? What are you thinking of? What have you made this with? Through what (means) has the man become so unhappy?

PAGE 75. No. 12.

Wer ist dieser Mann? Wer sind jene Damen? Von wem sprechen Sie? An wen schreiben Sie? Wovon reden Sie? Wer hat dies gethan? Wem haben Sie meinen Stock gegeben? Für wen arbeiten Sie? Was suchen Sie? Was hat er Ihnen geantwortet? Was haben Sie genommen? Was ist der Mensch ohne Vernunft? Wo ist die Luise? Weiß sie nicht, daß der Zeichenlehrer kommt? Was würde er sagen, wenn sie nicht hier wäre? Wer ist in meinem Zimmer gewesen? Wem haben Sie es gesagt? Von wem haben Sie es gehört? Durch welche Städte sind Sie gekommen? In welcher Schlacht ist Ihr Bruder verwundet geworden? Welcher Ihrer Brüder ist angekommen? Mit wel-

chem dieser Herren waren Sie in Paris? An welchen dieser Bedienten
haben Sie diesen Brief abgegeben?

PAGE 76. No. 13.

Here is the young man who has saved the child of our neighbor.
The house which you see down there, belongs to my aunt. The
apartments which I inhabit are very roomy. Do you know the
lady of whom we speak. Where is the poor boy, to whom you
have given the bread? The servant, to whom I had entrusted my
letters, has not returned. Have you seen the soldier, whose mother
has died? The young officer, whose bravery people praise so
much, is the son-in-law of my neighbor. The wine-merchant,
whom you have seen at my house, has sent me twelve bottles of
Bordeaux wine. The ribbons, which you have sent me, are too
wide. The days which I have spent with you, have been the most
agreeable of my life. There is the tree, under which we have
rested so often. These are precious stones, the value of which I
do not know. Here is the knife the point of which Charles has
broken. These are the gentlemen, to whom we have communicated the news.

PAGE 76. No. 14.

Da ist der kleine Knabe, der so schön schreibt. Das ist die junge Dame,
die mit vieler Leichtigkeit spricht. Ich liebe die Kinder nicht, die zu viel
sprechen. Das ist der Arzt, den ich gesehen habe, die Dame, welche Sie
kennen. Das sind die Bücher, welche Sie suchen. Wo ist der Brief, von
dem Sie sprechen? Das ist ein Mann, dessen Rechtlichkeit ich kenne.
Das ist nicht der Kaufmann, von dem wir unsere Bänder gekauft haben.
Sagen Sie mir, wem Sie meinen Stock gegeben haben. Wissen Sie,
wem dieser schöne Garten gehört? Ich weiß nicht, von welchem Garten
Sie sprechen. Sind das die Kinder deren Vater todt ist?

PAGE 76. No. 15.

Tell me what pleases you most (what you like best). Tell me
what he has told you. I do not know what you want (wish, desire).
Do you know what has happened to him? Give me what you have
promised me. Tell us what you think of it. Do not believe all
he says. He has not been willing to confide his grief to me, for
which I am very sorry. Here is what you demand. Take what
you please. He speaks of all (that) he hears. That is what I
rejoice at. That is not what I am thinking of. Have you heard
what he has said? Do you comprehend what he wants to say with
it? Always avoid what is injurious to health. Never speak of
what you do not understand.

Page 77. No. 16.

Ich habe verstanden, was Sie mir gesagt haben. Ich werde Ihnen geben, was ich Ihnen versprochen habe. Wissen Sie, was er will? Hat er Ihnen gesagt, was ihm begegnet ist? Wir sprechen nicht von Allem, was wir hören. Wir sagen nicht immer, was wir denken. Das ist Alles, was ich Ihnen sagen kann. Wissen Sie, woran ich denke, wovon ich spreche? Das ist es, worüber wir uns freuen. Das ist es, worüber ich betrübt bin und worüber ich mich beklage. Das, was schön ist, ist nicht immer nützlich.

Page 77. No. 17.

I have seen every thing. All this furniture is very beautiful. All my children are gone out. The whole garden is well planned (arranged). We have worked all day and all night. Mr. N. is the benefactor of all the distressed. We have communicated it to all those present. All our relations have left. All those who were here, have heard it. It is the same gentleman we have seen yesterday. It is always the same answer. He says always the same thing. I had the same thought; I wanted to do the same thing. Give me of the same cloth, of the same linen. We have sent it to the same merchant, we have said it to the same woman. He has applied to the same lawyer. I have heard it myself. We shall bring it to you ourselves. Tell it to him yourself.

Page 78. No. 18.

Alles ist verloren. Das ganze Land ist überschwemmt. Die Familie ist auf dem Lande. Alle Menschen sind sterblich. Alle meine Freunde sind angekommen. Ich sehe Sie alle Tage. Wir haben es selbst gesehen. Der König selbst hat davon gesprochen. Es ist derselbe Mann und dieselbe Frau. Es sind dieselben Kinder. Wir bewohnen dasselbe Haus. Sie sind immer Derselbe. Ich habe von derselben Tinte gekauft, von demselben Papier. Ich habe es demselben Bedienten gegeben. Meine Schwestern werden selbst kommen. Man muß nicht immer von sich selbst sprechen.

Page 78. No. 19.

Thou art taller than I; but thy brother is not so tall as I. My uncle is quite as rich as thy father. We have as many books as you; but we have not so many engravings and maps. My son, thou hast been so industrious that thou deservest a reward. I have not spent as much as you think. I am as rejoiced at it as you. Your sister has as fine clothes as mine. My sons do not work as much as yours. Mr. N. has more children than we; I think he has more (of them) than nine. Louisa has fewer friends than Henrietta. We have been more industrious to-day than yesterday; we have made two exercises more. I have much patience, but you have

4

still more (of it). Henry has copied more than ten letters to-day. You cannot give him less than two dollars.

PAGE 78. No. 20.

Iſt Ihr Bruder ſo groß als ich? Er iſt nicht ſo groß als Sie. Hat er ſo viele Bücher als ich? Er hat nicht ſo viele Bücher als Sie. Der junge Mann hat eben ſo ſchöne Kupferſtiche als Sie. Ich liebe ihn eben ſo ſehr, als Sie ihn lieben. Sie lieben mich nicht ſo ſehr, als ich Sie liebe. Ihr Vetter war ſo beſchäftigt, daß er mich nicht ſah. Ihr Arzt iſt glücklicher, aber nicht ſo geſchickt als der unſere. Dieſer Arzt iſt ſehr reich, er hat mehr als dreißig Häuſer. Dieſer Arbeiter verlangt nicht weniger als ſechs Thaler. Das Kind hat mehr als zwei Stunden geſchlafen. Unſer Gärtner hat viele Kinder, ich glaube, daß er deren mehr als neun hat. Wir haben heut drei Aufgaben mehr gemacht.

PAGE 79. No. 21.

I do not know what can be the matter with thee, my dear Julia: the more people laugh here, the more thou criest; the more one encouragest thee to give thyself up to joy, the more thou grievest. It is now a quarter of an hour since I have observed thee, and the more I look at thee, the less I can comprehend what makes thee weep so. Oh, dear uncle! you do not know all (that) I have to suffer; everybody has something against me, and the more I reflect on the treatment I suffer, the less I can comprehend what has brought it upon me. I was as happy in the country as I am unhappy in the town. You are as severe now as you were formerly indulgent. Thou art never satisfied, my child; the more thou hast, the more thou demandest. The less (one wishes) we wish, the more contented we are. The older we are, the more sensible we should be.

PAGE 79. No. 22.

So glücklich wir auf dem Lande waren, ſo unglücklich ſind wir in der Stadt. So fleißig dieſer junge Mann iſt, ſo faul iſt ſein Bruder. So lehrreich gute Bücher ſind, ſo ſchädlich ſind ſchlechte. So verſchwenderiſch Herr R. iſt, ſo geizig iſt ſein Onkel. Je mehr Geld man hat, deſto mehr Freunde hat man. Je mehr er trinkt, deſto durſtiger iſt er. Je weicher Federn ſind, deſto ſchlechter ſind ſie. Je weniger Wünſche man hat, deſto zufriedener iſt man. Je mehr man ihn bittet, deſto weniger thut er es. Je weniger Geld er hat, deſto ſparſamer iſt er. Je gelehrter wir ſind, deſto beſcheidener ſollten wir ſein.

PAGE 80. No. 23.

Every age has its duties. Every one has done his duty. Every tree, every plant, every animal is useful. We must well employ every day. This boy stands still at every house. Everybody has

his faults. I have presented a book to each. Do you know one
of these ladies? I know some of these gentlemen, but I know
none of these ladies. Do you eat some pears? There are beautiful apples; give me some. Somebody has told me, that you depart
to-morrow. We should (must) speak ill of no one. I cannot give
it to you, for I have promised it to some one. Nobody knows that
you are here. We have told it to nobody. I have lost none (not
one) of my books. I have nothing to do. We have not spoken
of any thing.

PAGE 80. No. 24.

Jeder Stand hat seine Annehmlichkeiten. Jeder Lärm schreckt ihn. Ich
habe es jedem Knaben und jedem Mädchen erzählt. Jeder muß einst
sterben. Der Fürst spricht mit Jedem seiner Unterthanen. Leihen Sie
mir einige Federn. Wir haben einige Studenten gesehen. Einige unse=
rer Freunde werden diesen Abend kommen. Ich werde einige Ihrer Bü=
cher nehmen. Niemand weiß es. Ich kenne Niemanden. Ich werde es
Niemanden sagen. Keiner meiner Freunde wird kommen. Kennen Sie
einige von diesen Damen? Ich kenne keine von ihnen. Ich habe mit
keinem von diesen Herren gesprochen. Ich spreche von Jemandem, den
Sie noch nicht gesehen haben. Ich habe meinen Regenschirm Jemandem
geliehen, der ihn mir morgen zurückgeben wird.

PAGE 80. No. 25.

He gives to one what he takes from the other. Both are wrong.
He has made reproaches to both, but neither the one nor the other
has deserved them. I have taken leave from both. This soldier
has lost both his legs. These two brothers love each other much;
they never go out without one another. They cannot separate.
Give me another hat and other gloves. Do not envy the happiness
of others. Speak to me of something else. I know nothing certain
about it. A certain gentleman and lady have told me of it. I have
heard it from several persons. It is rare that one has several
friends. I would lend thee a pen if I had several. We have spent
several days in this town. I tell it to everybody who will hear it.
We shall defend ourselves against everybody who will attack us.
The law will punish everybody who will not observe it.

PAGE 81. No. 26.

Die Sache ist noch nicht gewiß. Ein gewisser Knabe sagte es mir. Ich
habe Ihr Buch einem gewissen Schüler gegeben. Mein Vater wußte dar=
über noch nichts Gewisses. Mehre meiner Freunde wissen es. Ich habe
heute mehre Briefe erhalten. Ich habe es von mehren Personen gehört.
Geben Sie mir ein anderes Hemde und andere Strümpfe. Der Eine
sagt dieses, der Andere jenes. Haben Sie keine andere Tinte, keine an=

dern Federn? Diese beiden Knaben lieben einander; sie sind beide fleißig. Die Menschen müssen einander lieben. Diese beiden Freunde denken oft an einander. Jeder, der reich ist, sollte wohlthätig sein. Derjenige, welcher fleißig ist, hat keine Langeweile.

PAGE 81. No. 27.

I am going to-morrow to Aix la Chapelle. My father has already gone there yesterday. , I was not yet there. You have not gained anything by that; I will remain there three days. We spent the night there. I have promised him and I shall think of it. The ink was a little too thick. I have poured a little water into it. I am not used to it. Will you sit down upon this bench? Yes, I will sit down upon it. Is your father in the room? No, he is not there. What have you planted near your flowers? I have planted vegetables there. Charles has made ten mistakes, and I have made nine. Are you satisfied with my son? I am very well pleased with him. Have you spoken to the prince about my misfortune. I have not yet spoken to him about it. Have you received letters? Yes, I have received some. Will you have a glass of wine. I thank you, I have already drunk some. Have you any money? No, I have none. That is a good opportunity; I shall avail myself of it.

PAGE 82. No. 28.

Haben Sie Wein? Ich habe welchen, ich habe keinen. Hat Ihr Bruder Tinte? Er hat welche, er hat keine. Hast du Papier? Ich habe welches, ich habe keins. Haben diese Herren Pferde? Sie haben welche, sie haben keine. Hat Ihre Tante Schwestern? Sie hat zwei. Ist deine Cousine auf dem Ball gewesen? Sie ist nicht da gewesen. Ist Ihr Onkel auf das Land gegangen? Er ist diesen Morgen (heute Morgen) hingegangen. Wollen Sie an meine Angelegenheit denken? Ich werde daran denken. Wir werden viel dabei gewinnen. Der Wein ist zu stark; gießen Sie ein wenig Wasser dazu. Wie viele Fehler haben Sie gemacht? Ich habe deren sechs gemacht. Haben sie über den Krieg gesprochen? Ja, sie haben darüber gesprochen.

PAGE 82. No. 29.

You complain of the ingratitude of man. Yes, the most important services are sometimes very badly rewarded, and it happens very often that those, to whom one has done the greatest service, are the most ungrateful. Your neighbor Robert, for instance, is the most ungrateful man in the world. He finds a pleasure in slandering his benefactors. He has entertained me these days with the most absurd things, he spoke ill of the most respectable people, and gave himself up to the most absurd calumnies. He forgets that we have

rescued him out from the most frightful misery. That grieves
me more than you can imagine. Mr. Robert speaks differently
from what he thinks. He is not as malicious as you imagine. An
honest man does not speak otherwise than he thinks.

PAGE 82. No. 30.

Meine Schwester singt besser, als sie spielt. Sie sind glücklicher, als
Sie es verdienen. Die Damen sprechen gewöhnlich mehr, als sie schrei=
ben. Sie sind früher gekommen, als ich dachte. Herr N. ist der geschick=
teste Arzt, den ich kenne. Wir sprechen von dem geschicktesten Arzte der
Stadt. Sie klagen ihn des schrecklichsten Verbrechens an. Er hat mir
das bestimmteste Versprechen gegeben, an mich zu schreiben. Wir werden
den kürzesten Weg nehmen, um nach S. zu gehen. Ich erinnere mich noch
der wichtigsten Umstände. Ich war gestern in N.; es ist eine der merk=
würdigsten Städte in Europa. Wir haben unsere Freunde der unglück=
lichsten Lage entrissen.

PAGE 83. No. 31.

Sit down near me. Read to me, what you have written. Do
not fret any more about it. Learn to think before you write.
Arrange these letters before you go away. Do not eat any more
grapes, they are not yet ripe. Come here, my friend. Go there,
my dear. We will say no more about it. We will sit down to the
table. We will go walking a little. Let us pardon our enemies.
Let us go home. We will not remain any longer. Let us rather
go back to town. Come, children, it is already late. Do not run so
hard, Henry. You shall come no more, if you are not better.

PAGE 83. No. 32.

Laßt uns diesem armen kleinen Knaben ein Stück Brod geben. Sie
rufen uns, laßt uns hinuntergehen. Madam, nehmen Sie noch eine
Tasse Kaffee. Laßt uns die Zeitung vorher lesen. Laßt uns gegen Je=
den gerecht sein. Laßt uns die Tugend lieben und das Laster hassen. Laßt
uns ein wenig näher treten, kommen Sie ein wenig näher. Sehen Sie
hierher, mein Herr. Laßt uns immer hoffen. Laßt uns noch einen Au=
genblick warten. Gehen Sie noch nicht fort. Wascht euch, ehe ihr aus=
geht. Geh' zu Bett. Stehe nicht auf. Laßt uns jetzt arbeiten. Wir
wollen nicht mehr plaudern.

PAGE 83. No. 33.

I hate this man; he is a liar. We hate idleness. We shall always
hate those who are addicted to vice. I hate no one. God will not
have us hate any one. Hate lies, but do not hate your neighbor.
Shun the wicked, and seek the society of those who are virtuous.
This man is universally despised. Every one avoids him. We

avoid all those who give themselves up to idleness. My uncle has advised me to shun the company of these young people. Let us shun flatterers. Time flies, we must make use of it.

PAGE 84. No. 34.

Warum haffen Sie mich? Ich haffe Sie nicht. Wir müffen Niemanden haffen. Ich habe immer die Schmeichler gehaßt. Fliehe das Böfe und thue das Gute. Ich fliehe die fchlechte Gefellfchaft. Fliehe die Böfen. Laffet uns alle das Lafter fliehen. Ihre Schwefter muß den Umgang diefer Damen fliehen. Bleiben Sie; fliehen Sie nicht. Sie haben nichts zu fürchten. Jedermann flieht die Lügner. Wir müffen unfere Zeit benutzen. Wir verachten Diejenigen, die ihre Pflicht nicht erfüllen. Derjenige, welcher verachtet ift, ift unglücklich. Tugendhafte Leute find geliebt und geachtet.

PAGE 84. No. 35.

I have been occupied all the evening; I shall now dress myself. Wilt thou go walking to-day? I rejoice at the arrival of my father. Ennui is unknown to him who knows how to occupy himself. Charles has proposed to himself to go this afternoon to N. We shall make ourselves much pleasure there (shall have much amusement there). We are happy when we are well. Do not praise thyself; beware of arrogance. The wind abates, we shall have fine weather. Rest yourself a little. This pupil has improved. We have lost ourselves. You have exposed yourselves to a great danger. We should have incurred reproaches, if we had done so.

PAGE 84. No. 36.

Wafchen Sie fich. Sie haben fich noch nicht gewafchen. Ich habe mich diefen Morgen gewafchen. Wollen Sie fich nicht wafchen? Worüber freuen Sie fich? Ich freue mich, Sie zu fehen. Wir freuen uns über Ihr Glück. Ich kann mich nicht mehr freuen. Meine Schweftern haben fich vorgenommen, auf den Ball zu gehen. Diefer Hund hat fich verirrt. Ich werde mich diefer Gefahr nicht ausfetzen. Womit befchäftigen Sie fich? Ich befchäftige mich mit Lefen. Sie werden fich Vorwürfe zuziehen, wenn Sie nicht hingehen. Hüten Sie fich, das zu thun. Mein Vetter wird fich niemals beffern. Wir haben uns geftern fehr vergnügt. Luife ift noch nicht angezogen. Sie irren fich, fie ift fchon in die Kirche gegangen.

PAGE 85. No. 37.

Sit down my child. I am not tired; I seldom sit down. Sit down; I shall sit down also. Do not sit down upon that chair, it is broken. We will sit down upon this bench. Louisa and Henrietta, come, and seat yourselves along side of me. Why do you not sit down? I have sat too long, I can sit no longer. It is impossible

for me to sit the whole day. Where is thy brother? He is sitting
before the door. The whole family was sitting round the table.
My father wants me to sit always. Gentlemen, why do you stand?
Sit down. I cannot stand long, I get tired immediately. I have
been standing here an hour, waiting for thee. Where is thy dog,
Charles? He is lying behind the stone. My cousin yesterday was
lying in bed as late as ten o'clock. We have been lying in the
grass until now.

PAGE 85. No. 38.

Setzen Sie sich gefälligst. Ich bitte, setzen Sie sich. Ich habe mich
schon gesetzt. Ich setze mich, wo ich Platz finde. Wollen Sie sich nicht
setzen? Ich werde mich an Ihre Seite setzen. Machen Sie Platz, damit
dieser Herr sich setzen kann. Sie sitzen nicht gut, mein Fräulein. Ich saß
dort nicht gut; ich habe zwischen Ihren beiden Schwestern gesessen. Wo
saßen Sie in der Kirche? Wir saßen im Chor. Diese Herren stehen
immer; bitte sie, sich zu setzen. Ich habe eine ganze Stunde gestanden.

PAGE 85. No. 39.

Do you know when you were born? I was born in the month
of May. Every man is born in order to die. This boy was born
after the death of his father. I like this book. I should like this
garden better, if it were larger. My hat will please you (you will
like my hat). How do you like this place? I like it very well.
I should however like it still better, if I had some friends with me,
but my friends do not like the country. I have always liked the
country better than the town. Why are you silent? I cannot be
silent, when I see something that displeases me. A young person
ought always to be silent, when older persons speak together. Be
silent, I will hear no more of it.

PAGE 86. No. 40.

Wann sind Sie geboren? Ich bin im Monat September geboren. Cor-
neille ist in Rouen geboren. Wir sind alle geboren, um zu sterben. Ich
bin geboren, um unglücklich zu sein. Diese Dame gefällt mir sehr. Auf
dem Lande gefällt es mir nicht. Es gefällt mir weit besser in der Stadt.
Gefällt Ihnen dieser Ort? (Gefallen Sie sich hier?) Wir gefallen uns
hier besser als in unserm Hause. Kommen Sie gefälligst hierher. Das
hat mir nicht gefallen. Schweigen Sie. Meine Tante kann nicht schweigen. Wir schweigen, wenn jede Dame spricht. Ich werde nicht schweigen.
Ich habe zu lange geschwiegen. Warum haben Sie geschwiegen? Wenn
ich geschwiegen hätte, würde ich besser gethan haben.

PAGE 86. No. 41.

Next to God, thy parents are thy greatest benefactors. I go to
London to-morrow and shall only return in three weeks. Which

way must we go, to get to yonder castle? I shall come to your
house after supper. This picture is painted from nature. Mr. N.
was here and has inquired after you. According to all appearances,
thou wilt lose thy law-suit. According to my opinion, I shall gain
it. These goods are sold by the yard. Your brother is always
dressed in the fashion (fashionably). You do not keep time when
you dance. I have advised you to save in order to grow rich by
degrees; but you continue to live always the same. I inhabit a
room, which looks into the garden. According to what your brother
has told me, you are very well satisfied with your teacher. After
having waited an hour we went away.

PAGE 86. No. 42.

I was this morning at the Prussian ambassador's. He was in a
very good humor, took me by the hand and assured me, that this
very day he would make inquiry at the minister's respecting my
affairs. I found him at dinner, and thought to myself that he
would not receive my visit. I had an important letter with me,
which I handed to him. Have you any money about you? At
whose house do you live? I live near the church, not far from the
post-office. Take hold of the knife by the handle and not by the
blade. The one took hold of him by the head, the other by the
legs. I assure you upon my honor. I met him on coming out of
the theatre. We shall tell him when an opportunity offers. Why
do you sit by the fire, are you not well? Put the goods aside for
me, I shall send for them. My brother perished at the battle of
Leipzig. At these words, he burst into tears. We were always
together, night and day. It was an ancient custom with the
Romans, to send presents to their friends on their birthdays.

PAGE 87. No. 43.

With whom have you been walking? With what lady have
you danced? Always act with prudence, defend yourself with
courage. Beauty vanishes with age (with the years). Is your gun
loaded with a bullet? Your friend has honored me with a visit.
People are (one is) very well satisfied with him. He arrived yesterday with the stage. He wears a brown coat with golden buttons.
The young man with the long hair is the son of the house. Have
you seen the man with the large nose and the black eyes? My
child, thou must eat thy meat with the fork and not with thy hand.
My cousin has told me, with tears in her eyes, that she must depart
to-morrow. This landscape is drawn with a pencil and not with
a pen. I cannot accept this present with a good conscience. He

came in with a pistol in his hand and cried with a loud voice. In German every substantive is written with a capital letter.

PAGE 88. No. 44.

What are you doing? I am translating from German into French. Where do you come from? We come from school, from (out of) the garden. Where are you from? I am from Berlin, and my friend is from Lyons. Who has drunk out of thy glass? I know it from (by) experience. I have done it with a good intention, out of love for him. I see from your letter that you continue to be unwell. The cholera comes from Asia. This statue is of marble. These hats are out of fashion. He screams as loud as he can. I love him from my heart. My brother has not left his room for the last week. Go out of my sight, envy speaks out of you. I have not played the piano this long time; I am getting out of practice. The light is out. With death all is to an end. The pupil must work voluntarily, not from fear of punishment, else he will go to school from one end of the year to the other (year after year), without making any great progress.

PAGE 88. No. 45.

Until we meet again! Yes, certainly at the ball we shall meet again. Nothing in the world I like better than a ball. I believe thee on thy word. But do not too much anticipate this pleasure, it might be easily put off for a fortnight. My brothers are going a'hunting to-morrow, and I shall go into the country. Sit down upon a chair, and do not mount the ladder. We have lent him this sum on his honest face. He advanced towards me and wanted to force me to follow him. I hear a noise in the street, they have caught a thief in the act (of stealing). My mother left a quarter to seven. What is this flower called in German? Are you angry with me? How many Groshen are there in a dollar? I shall depart for a short time. But at all events I shall be back by the fifteenth of this month. At most I shall remain till the twentieth. You may do it at my risk. I have (bade him farewell) taken leave of him for ever. It is true, he still relies upon me, but I have told him that he needs no longer count upon me.

PAGE 89. No. 46.

There is a thunder-storm over the town. That sword was suspended over his head. Our cousin is always sitting over his books. His hair was hanging over his eyes. The perspiration was streaming over his forehead. He is in debt over head and ears. That is beyond his strength, beyond his understanding. These young people always fall asleep, when they are reading (over their book). My wife is upwards of fifty and I am upwards of sixty years old. This cloth is more than two yards wide. We must go over this river, over this bridge. I shall go to Leipsic by the way of Frankfort. Honor before riches. This day week my father will arrive. He has been absent more than six months. Thy cousin owes me more than a hundred dollars. Do not rejoice too early at the success of thy undertaking; thou art not yet (over the mountain) out of the woods. It is raining very hard, we have got wet through and through. Thy friend writes us no more; in the beginning we received letters upon letters from him.

Page 89. No. 47.

This general bears arms against his fatherland. He who acts against his conscience acts against God and the law. I admire his love towards his family and his faithfulness towards his friends. Our princess is benevolent towards the poor. Coriolanus was ungrateful to his country. He has been set at liberty on promising not to set his foot again in the country. I have paid him on his receipt. I'll bet ten to one, that he will not return. This service is nothing (compared with) to that one you have rendered me. This village lies to the north. He fell asleep towards two o'clock, and rose again towards nine o'clock. My grand-child will arrive towards the end of the winter.

Page 90. No. 48.

I shall certainly reward him, if I am satisfied with him. I shall tell you, when you come to (me) my house. Let me know when you will come. When you are happy remember the services we have rendered you. If I knew when he would come back, I should tell you. If my sister is wise she will follow your advice. When she is older, and shall have acquired a little more experience, she will find that I was right. I do not know if that is true. He asks whether you will start to-morrow? I cannot go out because the physician has forbidden it. I will lend you an amusing book, because you cannot go out. He works industriously, while his brother is walking about. He is daily praised by his teacher, whilst his brother is always blamed by them.

Page 90. No. 49.

As I cannot receive his visit to-day, I shall invite him for next Sunday. As I must depart to-morrow, I have come to take leave of you. As my father is ill, I cannot go walking. Because we feared to awaken you, we spoke low. As we were accustomed to live together, we had much trouble to separate. When Pelopidas reproached Epaminondas, that he did not leave any children to the state, the latter answered: "Thou dost still less for thy fatherland, as thou wilt only leave to it a profligate son." When Titus had allowed a day to pass, without doing any good to any body, he said: "I have lost a day."

PAGE 90. No. 50.

The children of my neighbor are so stubborn that they will never fulfil the commands of their parents. When the father wishes to take them for a walk, they want to stay at home; and when the mother wishes them to work, they want to go out. It is cold, we will go into the house, or we will play a little, to warm ourselves. Religion demands, that we shall not do unto another what we do not wish others to do unto us. These plants require a moist soil and particular attention. We can do much, if we wish. We shall not be able to undertake this journey, because the season is already too far advanced. Whoever wants to travel profitably, must know the language of the country in which he travels. Can you skate? I could skate formerly, but since I broke my leg, I can do it no longer. I have had a pair of new boots made. This teacher permits his pupils to go out as often as they please.

DIVERSE EXERCISES.

PAGE 92.

1. THE CANE-PIPE.

A king had a treasurer, who from being a shepherd (from the shepherd's staff), had raised himself to this important office. The treasurer, however, was accused before the king, that he was robbing the royal treasure, and that he concealed the stolen jewels in a vault, which was provided with an iron door.

The king paid a visit to the treasurer, looked at his palace, and when he came to the iron door he ordered it to be opened. When the king went in, he was quite astonished. He saw nothing but the four walls, a rustic table, and a rushbottomed chair. On the table lay a shepherd's pipe, a staff, and a pouch.

But the treasurer spoke: "In my youth I minded the sheep. Thou, o king, drewest me to thy court. In this vault I have since spent an hour daily; with pleasure have I thought of my former station, and have repeated the songs which I sang formerly in praise of the Lord, when peacefully I tended my flock. Oh, let me return to my native fields, where I was happier than at thy court!"

The king was very angry with those who had calumniated the good man; he embraced him, and requested him to remain with him.

PAGE 92.

2. THE THREE ROBBERS.

Three robbers murdered and plundered a merchant, who with a quantity of money and jewels travelled through a forest. They carried the stolen treasure into their cave, and sent the youngest of them into the town, to buy victuals.

When he was gone, the other two said: "Why shall we share these great riches with this lad? When he comes back we will kill him." The young robber thought to himself on the way: "How happy should I be, if all this money belonged to me! I will poison my two companions, and I shall keep it all to myself." When he had arrived in town, he bought victuals, put poison into the wine, and returned into the forest.

Scarcely had he entered the cave, when the two others rushed at him, and pierced him with their daggers. Hereupon they sat down, ate and drank the poisoned wine. They died in violent pains, and people found their bodies in the midst of the treasures, which they had accumulated.

PAGE 93.

3. THE PILGRIM.

In a very magnificent castle of which every trace has been lost long ago, there lived once a very rich knight. He spent much money to embellish it, but did little for the poor.

There came once a poor pilgrim, who asked a night's lodging. The knight insolently sent him away, saying: "This castle is not an inn." "Allow me only three questions," said the pilgrim, "and I will proceed (on my journey)." "Agreed," replied the knight. "Who inhabited this castle before you?" asked the pilgrim. "My father." "Who before him was the inhabitant of this castle?" "My grand-father." "And who will live in it after you?" "My son, please God." "Well," said the pilgrim, "if each lives in it only a certain time, and one must always make room for the other in it, you are only guests here, and the castle is really an inn."

Therefore do not spend so much to adorn this house, which you only possess for a short time. Rather do good to the poor, and you will obtain an everlasting dwelling in heaven."

The knight took these words to heart, granted the pilgrim's request, and in future was more benevolent towards the poor.

PAGE 93.
4. THE ROBIN-REDBREAST.

A robin-redbreast came in the severest part of the winter to the window of a pious farmer, as if it wished to come in. Then the farmer opened his window and took the confiding little animal kindly into his dwelling. Now it picked up the scraps and crumbs, which fell from his table, and the children of the farmer liked the little bird very much.

But when the spring came again into the land, and the bushes covered with foliage, the farmer opened his window, and the little guest flew into the neighboring forest, and built its nest and sung its cheerful song.

And behold, when the winter returned, the robin-redbreast came again to the dwelling of the farmer, and brought its little mate with it. But the farmer and his little children rejoiced much, when they saw the little animals, which looked around so trustfully. And the children said : " The birds look at us, as if they wished to say something to us."

Then answered the father: "If they could speak, they would say: Confidence awakens confidence and love begets a return of love."

PAGE 94.
5. THE VOICE OF JUSTICE.

A rich man, named Chryses, ordered his servants to expel a poor widow together with her children from her dwelling, because she was not able to pay the customary rent. When the servants came, the woman said: "Oh, tarry a little; perhaps your master may take pity on us, I will go to him and implore him."

Thereupon the widow went with her four children to the rich man, one of them was lying sick, and all prayed not to expel them. But Chryses spoke: "I cannot alter my commands, unless you pay your debt immediately."

Then the mother wept bitterly, and said: "Oh, the nursing of a sick child has consumed all my earnings, and has prevented my working." And the children prayed with the mother not to expel them.

But Chryses turned away from them and went to his summer-house, and laid himself down upon the cushion, to rest, as he was in the habit of doing. It was however a sultry day, and close to the garden-saloon flowed a river, which spread coolness, and it was so still, that not a breath of air was stirring.

Then Chryses heard the rustling of the reeds on the shore, but it sounded to him like the whining of the children of the poor widow; and he became uneasy on his pillow.

Then he hearkened to the murmuring of the stream, and it appeared to him as if he reposed on the shore of an immense ocean, and he rolled on his pillow.

And when he listened again, there resounded from the distance, the thunder of a storm, and he thought he heard the voice of judgment.

He now arose suddenly, hastened to the house, and ordered his servants, to open the house for the poor widow. But she had gone with her children into the forest, and was nowhere to be found. In the mean time the storm had risen, and it thundered and there fell a violent rain. Chryses however was gloomy in his mind, and he wandered about.

The next day Chryses learned, that the sick child had died in the forest, and that the mother had moved away with the others. And he became disgusted with his garden, the pavilion and the cushions, and enjoyed no longer the cool of the murmuring stream.

Soon after Chryses fell sick, and in the heat of the fever he always heard the whispering of the reeds and the murmuring river and the hollow roaring of the thunderstorm. Thus he expired.

PAGE 95.

6. THE PEACHES.

A farmer brought with him from the town five peaches, the most beautiful that could be seen. His children, however, saw this fruit for the first time; therefore they wondered and rejoiced much at the beautiful apples with the red cheeks and delicate down. Then the father divided them between his four boys, and one the mother received.

In the evening when the children were going into the bed-room, the father asked them: "Well, how did you find the taste of the beautiful apples?"

"Exquisite, dear father," said the eldest. "It is a beautiful fruit, so tart and so mild of taste. I have carefully preserved the kernel, and will raise a tree from it."

"Bravo!" said the father. "That we call taking care of the future as it becomes a farmer."

"I have eaten mine immediately," exclaimed the youngest, "and have thrown away the kernel, and mother has given me the half of hers. Oh, it tasted so sweet, and melts in one's mouth!"

"Well," said the father, "it is true, you have not acted very prudently, but naturally and in a childlike manner; for prudence there is still room enough in life."

Then the second son began: "I have picked up the stone which my little brother had thrown away, and have broken it open. But there was a kernel in it, which tasted as sweet as a nut. But my peach I have sold, and received so much money for it, that I can, when I go to town, buy perhaps a dozen for it."

The father shook his head, and said: "This, no doubt, is shrewd, but it was not childlike and natural. Heaven preserve you from becoming a merchant!"

"And you, Edmund?" asked the father. Unembarrassed and frankly Edmund answered: "I have taken my peach to the son of our neighbor, poor George, who has the fever. He would not take it, but I have laid it upon his bed, and have come away."

"Well," said the father, "and who has made the best use of his peach?"

Then all three exclaimed: "It is brother Edmund who has done it!" and the mother embraced him with a tear in her eye.

PAGE 96.
7. THE DESERT ISLAND.

A rich and benevolent man wished to make one of his slaves happy: he gave him his liberty, and had a ship freighted with many costly goods. "Go," said he, "sail to a foreign land, sell these goods, and all the profit shall be thine." The slave departed; but scarcely had he been for any time at sea, when a violent storm arose, and cast the ship against a cliff, where it was wrecked. The costly goods sank into the sea, all his companions perished, and he reached with difficulty the shore of an island. Hungry, naked and without help, he went deeper into the land and wept over his misfortune, when he saw at a distance a large city, from which a great number of inhabitants came to meet him with loud cries: "Hail, our king!" they shouted, placed him on a splendid carriage and conducted him into the city. He arrived at the royal palace, where they put a purple robe on him, bound a diadem round his brow, and made him ascend a golden throne. The gentry surrounded him, fell down before him, and, in the name of the whole nation took the oath of fidelity.

The new king believed in the beginning that all this was but a beautiful dream, until the continuation of his happiness allowed him to doubt no longer that the wonderful event was really true. "I do not comprehend," said he to himself, "what has bewitched the eyes of this strange people, to make a naked stranger their king. They do not know who I am, do not ask where I came from, and place me upon their throne! What peculiar custom is that in this country?"

PAGE 96.

8. CONTINUATION.

Thus he thought, and became so curious to know the cause of his elevation, that he determined to ask one of the noblemen of his court, who appeared to him to be a wise man, for the solution of this riddle. "Vizier!" he addressed him, "why have you made me your king? How could you know that I had arrived in your island? And what will at last become of me?" "My lord!" answered the vizier, "this island is inhabited by spirits. A long time ago, they implored the Almighty to send them every year a son of Adam, that he might govern them. The Almighty has granted their request, and every year on the same day causes a man to land on their island. The inhabitants, as thou hast seen, joyfully hasten to meet him, and acknowledge him as their Lord; but his government only continues a year. When that time has elapsed, and the fixed day has appeared again, he is deprived of his dignity; they take from him his royal ornaments, and put on him bad clothes. His servants carry him by force to the shore, and place him in a vessel expressly built for that purpose, which carries him to another island. This island is void and a desert; he, who a few days before was a mighty king, arrives here naked and finds neither friends nor subjects. Nobody has compassion on his misfortunes, and he must lead in this desert land a sad and mournful life, if he has not made a wise use of his year. After the banishment of the old king, the people go to meet the new one, whom Providence sends them every year without exception, in the usual manner, and receive him with the same joy as the former. This, Sir! is the eternal law of this realm, which no king can repeal during his reign." "And have my predecessors," continued the king, "been informed of the short duration of their elevation?" "Not one of them has been unacquainted with this law of the perishableness (of their grandeur); but some allowed themselves to be blinded by the splendor, which surrounded their throne; they forgot the sad future, and spent their year without being wise. Others were intoxicated with the sweetness of their happiness, they dared not think of the desert island, for fear of embittering the pleasure of the present enjoyment; and thus they reeled, like drunken men, from pleasure to pleasure, until their time was past, and they were thrown into the ship. When the fatal day arrived, they all commenced to complain and to regret their blindness; but then it was too late, and they were exposed without mercy to the misery, which awaited them, and which they had not been willing to avoid by wisdom."

PAGE 97.

9. CONTINUATION.

This narrative of the spirit filled the king with fear; he shuddered at the fate of the former kings and wished to escape their misfortune. He saw with terror, that several of the weeks of his short year had already passed, and that it was necessary to make the better use of the remaining days of his reign. "Wise vizier," said he to the spirit, "thou hast revealed to me my future fate and the short duration of my royal power, but pray, tell me also what I must do to avoid the wretchedness of my predecessors?" "Remember, my lord!" answered the spirit, "that thou hast come naked to our island; for in the same manner, thou wilt leave it again and wilt never return. There is therefore but one means to prevent the want which threatens thee in that country of banishment, namely to make it fruitful and settle inhabitants upon it. This, according to our laws, is allowed, and thy subjects are so very obedient to thee, that they go wherever thou sendest them. Therefore send over a number of laborers to change these desert lands into fertile fields; build towns and stores, and provide them with all the necessaries of life. In one word, prepare a new empire for thyself, whose inhabitants will receive thee with joy, when thou shalt be banished. But hasten, let not a moment pass unemployed; for the time is short and the more thou doest for the cultivation of thy future abode, the more happy will thy stay be there. Imagine thy year to be already to an end to-morrow, and employ thy liberty, like a wise fugitive, who wants to escape from ruin. If thou despisest my counsel, or hesitatest thou art lost, and **a long state** of misery is thy lot."

The king was a wise man and the speech of the spirit lent wings to his activity. He immediately dispatched a number of his subjects, they went with pleasure and began the work with zeal. The island commenced to improve, and before six months had passed cities already stood in blooming fields. But notwithstanding the king's zeal did not abate; he sent over more and more inhabitants; those who followed were still more happy than the first, when they were going to so well cultivated a country, inhabited by their friends and relations.

PAGE 98.

10. THE END.

In the mean time the end of the year drew nigh. The former kings had trembled, when this moment approached; this one looked forward to it with impatience; for he was going into a land, where by a wise activity, he had built for himself a lasting mansion. At last, the wished for day arrived. The king was seized in his palace, was deprived of his diadem and of his royal robes, and was carried to the unavoidable ship, which brought him to his place of banishment. But scarcely had he landed on the shore of the new island, when the inhabitants hastened to meet him with joy, received him with great honor, and placed on his head, instead of that diadem, the glory of which had only lasted a year, an unfading wreath of flowers. The Almighty rewarded his wisdom: He bestowed upon him the immortality of his subjects, and made him their king for ever.

The rich and benevolent man is God; the slave, whom his master sends away, is man when born; the island, where he lands, is the world; the inhabitants who meet him with joy, are the parents who take care of the naked, weeping creature. The vizier, who informs him of the fate which is in store for him, is wisdom. The year of his reign, is the human life, and the desert island to which he is conducted, is the future world. The workmen, he sends there, are the good works, which he performs during his life. But the kings, who have gone there before him, without reflecting on the misfortune, which threatened them, are those foolish men, who only occupied themselves with earthly pleasures without thinking of their life after death, they are punished by eternal misery, because they appear before the Almighty with hands void of good works.

www.ingramcontent.com/pod-product-compliance
Lightning Source LLC
Chambersburg PA
CBHW021515090426
42739CB00007B/620